Rediscovering the Impact of Jesus' Death

Clues From the Gospel Audiences

Joseph A. Grassi

Sheed & Ward

Sheed & Ward TM is a service of National Catholic Reporter Pub-
lishing, Inc.

Library of Congress Catalog Card Number: 87-60873

ISBN: 1-55612-065-6

Published by:

Sheed & Ward
115 E. Armour Blvd. P.O. Box 414292
Kansas City, MO 64141-0281

To order, call: (800)821-7926

Contents

Introduction

One of the most exciting results of modern biblical research has been the rediscovery of the dramatic genre of Matthew, Mark, Luke and John. This has shown that the gospels were never really meant to be read *silently* by anyone. They were composed to be *read aloud* by a skilled performer to a live audience. They were considered a live performance in the same way that we regard a movie, a stage drama, or opera. Today, people come to such performances hoping for a total personal experience that will provide entertainment as well as possibly transform their lives through new insights. The same was true in ancient times. A live reading such as the gospels was believed to be filled with energy that could move people emotionally and help them change their lives.

In other words, the gospels were meant to be dramatic performances. The following are some of the characteristics of such works: they have a unified plot that leads to a definite conclusion; they have consistent characters that play their part in bringing out the full emotional impact of the whole narrative; they usually have heroes or heroines about which the story revolves; the composer presents the drama in a skilled, planned fashion so that the audience can identify with the whole story and become deeply involved in it; the drama must be understood as a whole, not piecemeal, since each scene, each actor, each utterance makes a definite contribution toward a climactic ending.

In the gospels, the hero and most important character is Jesus. All the gospel events lead to his death and its significance. Consequently, each gospel author has skilfully composed and arranged his libretto so that each part of it leads to the final death scene and conclusion. This means that each passage must be interpreted in the light of this final climax, just as each part of a movie, opera, or theatre drama is not to be understood piece by piece but finds its meaning in the total plot and ending.

By the "gospel audience" in my title, I mean primarily what many biblical scholars call "the implicit gospel audience." This means an ideal audience in the author's mind, who would listen to the gospel and respond to it in a desired way. This "ideal audience" does not always correspond to an actual audience either in ancient times or today. However, the gospels have been fruitfully read and re-read countless times through the centuries. This shows that the author's message, which he considered God's powerful word, still continues to stir the hearts of human beings who listen to it with the same openness and faith as the original audience. As readers go through this book they will find frequent transition notes to bridge the gap between ancient and modern audiences.

This book has made use of many scholarly contributions to the gospels' understanding, especially in regard to literary and rhetorical criticism. For easier reading, I have omitted all footnotes designating particular studies to which I am endebted. However, the bibliography at the end gives full information on scholars' works mentioned in the book and special sources I have used.

To rediscover the meaning of the gospels, we must again become part of the audience and find how each gospel author intended the death of Jesus to be understood by, and participated in, by those who listened to it. My purpose in this book is to facilitate this discovery.

1

Mark

The Blood of Martyrs
Is the Seed of Saints

By implied audience in Mark and throughout this book, I mean a group of people to whom the author directed his gospel in view of a suggested or ideal planned response. This description is similar to that of the ideal reader presented by D. Rhoads. It presupposes that Mark's gospel was composed as a dramatic narrative designed to draw the reader/audience toward a unified, desired conclusion or effect. A narrative dramatic view of the gospel has the following characteristics:

> The study of narrative emphasizes the unity of the final text. . .the narrator's point of view in telling the story is consistent throughout. The plot is coherent: events that are anticipated come to pass; conflicts are resolved; predictions are fulfilled. The characters are consistent from one scene to the next, fulfilling the roles they take on and the tasks they adopt. (Rhoads & Michie, 3)

From a narrative viewpoint, the most important character and hero in Mark is Jesus. He is the evident model for the audience as well as his disciples, to whom his first words are addressed:

1

"Come follow me" (1:17). The end result envisioned is that they will become "fishers of men" (1:17b). As a drama, the whole narrative leads up to the death of its hero Jesus, especially his last words and actions along with their immediate consequences. In parallel to the opening gospel call, following Jesus as far as the cross seems to be the ultimate response of the disciple as well as audience.

To identify the audience, we should know more about their situation and problems. These we will outline after presenting Mark's description of Jesus' death and before we try to assess the effect it would have on that audience.

> There was darkness over the whole earth until the ninth hour. And at the ninth hour Jesus cried with a loud voice, "Eloi, Eloi, lama sabachthani?" which means, "My God, my God, why has thou forsaken me?" And some of the bystanders, hearing it said, "Behold, he is calling Elijah." And one ran and, filling a sponge full of vinegar, put it on a reed and gave it to him to drink, saying, "Wait, let us see whether Elijah will come to take him down." (15:33-36)

From the viewpoint of narrative drama, the darkness over the whole earth from the sixth to ninth hour sets the scene for Jesus' darkest hour. His last words are written in Aramaic for special emphasis, "Eloi, Eloi, lama sabachthani" (15:34). Regardless of whether these words are a direct quotation of Ps 22:1 or not, they do convey the feeling of a final stage of abandonment: Judas, one of the twelve has betrayed Jesus; his male disciples have all fled at his arrest; Peter the rock has three times denied that he knew him; now it appears that even God has forsaken him. Jesus' words are even crudely misunderstood by some bystanders who think he is calling upon Elijah. The last words Jesus hears seem also to be a jeering remark: "Wait, let us see whether Elijah will come to take him down" (15:36). The words would be especially tormenting in view of the common belief that Elijah stood by the just in their last moments and helped them.

However, the description of Jesus' last actions and their consequences ends in a surprising and unexpected way:

> But Jesus uttered a loud cry and expired. Then the temple veil was torn in two from top to bottom. When the centurion facing opposite him saw how he had thus (cried out and) died, he said, "Truly this man was the (or a) son of God." (15:37-39)

The text seems to highlight this last cry of Jesus before his death. It is mentioned twice, the second in most texts of 15:39. Even if it is not original in the second text, the large number of manuscripts containing it suggest early interpretation of the cry as being the reason for the centurion's amazement and declaration. What would the centurion (and the gospel audience) have understood through this cry?

F. C. Grant suggested that this loud cry, *phonēn megalēn*, is the final great shout of a triumphant hero, citing the Greek OT uses of the phrase. S. Johnson added the note that Ignatius used the same expression in writing to the Philadelphians, "I cried out while I was with you, I spoke with a great voice, with God's own voice" (vii,1). It should be added that the NT elsewhere often has people, demons or angels speak with a "loud voice" to emphasize power or confidence. For example, Mark 1:26; 5:7; Luke 1:42; 17:15; 19:37; John 11:43, where Jesus calls forth Lazarus from the dead with a loud voice; Acts 7:60, where the final loud voice and prayer of Stephen seems parallel to that of Jesus; also, 14:10; 16:28; 19:28,34. The Apocalypse also uses the same expression, a great or loud voice, some 16 times to emphasize power.

The unusual tearing of the temple veil precedes the centurion's exclamation. As F. Matera has pointed out, this tearing may have several meanings depending on whether it was the outer veil of the holy place or the inner veil separating it from the holy of holies. Even for a non-Jewish audience, the torn veil would symbolize the breakdown of exclusive Jewish access to God, since the triumphant Roman celebration of their victory over Jerusalem in 71 A.D. included a representation of this veil. D. Juel has carefully traced the temple theme in Mark and shown how it leads to the tearing of the veil in 15:38 and the following confession of the centurion.

The careful listener in Mark's audience would be well aware that Jesus had already announced that the Temple's exclusiveness would be changed into a "house of prayer for all the nations" (11:17). However, the outer veil was not the most important one; the priests went in and out of it constantly each day to perform their functions in the holy place. Familiar with the scriptures, the Markan audience would know that the most important veil was the inner one, behind which the high priest entered once a year to sprinkle blood on the ark for the atonement of sins according to the ritual of Leviticus 16:19-34. This atonement was the great exclusive privilege of the Jewish people.

Since this atonement was exclusive for the Jews, the centurion could not participate in it unless the barrier of the veil was broken and access extended to others. To make this possible, the death of Christ is connected to the tearing of the temple veil and the centurion's "conversion"; otherwise he could hardly confess Jesus to be son of God, as the first person to do so in Mark's gospel. It is toward this confession that the whole gospel has been pointing. H. L. Chronis has noted the close textual connection between the tearing of the veil and the centurion's statement: The movement of the whole Markan drama is directed toward the son of God confession: the Greek passive voice *eschisthe* to describe the veil tearing and the emphatic, redundant "from top to bottom" (15:38) point to God's special action. The same verb describes the opening of the heavens at the dramatic epiphany at Jesus' baptism where the voice from heaven proclaims Jesus to be God's son. A similar theophany with the same voice occurs at Mark's midpoint transfiguration story (9:7).

In addition, the unusual description of the centurion as facing the dying Jesus, *ex anantias autou* (15:39) may have a cultic nuance in view of idiomatic expressions used for entering the temple and standing in the presence of the deity. This suggests that the God whose presence was veiled in the Temple now reveals himself through Jesus' death on the cross. Thus Chronis writes, "In his death, which culminates his mission of rejection and suffering (and thus satisfies the need for secrecy), Jesus manifests his true identity; and the effect, according to Mark, is equivalent to God himself showing his 'face' " (Chronis, 110). This view brings out the connection between the destruction of the Temple and Jesus' revelation of his identity:

> According to Mark, it is Jesus — suffering, dying, rising — who is the true locus of the divine "presence," not the *sanctum sanctorum* of the Temple! Mark links Jesus' death (and the rejection and suffering leading to that death) with the end of the temple because the revelation of God's "face" *on the cross* shatters the Jewish cultus at its very foundation: worship "before the face" i.e., *in the temple*. (Chronis, 111)

Thus we have strong links between Christ's death, the tearing of the veil and the centurion's confession, as bringing out the climax of the gospel. The gospel audience would have traced this process through the gospel drama. However, would they have understood *how* Jesus' death accomplished this? Of course, if they understood it as a sacrifice, there would be no difficulty. Yet studies on the supposed sacrificial terminology in Mark do not lead us to conclude that the audience would infer this immediately, despite texts like the Son of Man offering his life in ransom for many (10:45) and the last supper blood of the covenant poured out for the many (14:24).

Despite the inconclusiveness of sacrifical terminology, there are two factors which would have led the Markan audience to conclude that Jesus' death had a causative effect on the centurion's confession: The first factor is the essential language of obedience in the Scriptures that made any cultic action effective. For example, the effectiveness of the day of atonement rituals for forgiveness came from the fact that God commanded their performance and prescribed every detail. The ritual concludes with the words,

> And this shall be an everlasting statute for you, that
> atonement may be made for the people of Israel once
> in the year because of all their sins. And Moses did as
> the LORD commanded him. (Lev 16:34)

Similar words conclude the prescribed passover rituals: "Thus did all the people; as the LORD commanded Moses and Aaron, so they did" (Exod 12:50). Likewise, it was Abraham's obedience to the voice of God, not the actual offering of his son Isaac, that was the essential matter. God swore to bless Abraham and fulfill his promises using these words, "because you have obeyed my voice" (Gen 22:18).

Mark makes it very clear for his audience that Jesus' death came about through such obedience to God. For example, Jesus predicts three times his coming suffering and death (8:31; 9:31; 10:32-33). The use of the word *dei*, it is necessary, in the first prediction implies that he is fulfilling a divine plan; in addition, Jesus' knowledge of the future suggests some kind of hidden plan of God. Judas' initiative in bringing about Jesus' death is attributed to such a scriptural divine plan when Jesus says, "The Son of Man goes as it is written of him, but woe to that man by whom the Son of man is betrayed" (14:21).

This obedience emphasis is especially evident before Jesus' arrest when he prays for the strength to do the will of the Father, repeating the words, "Not what I will but what you will" (14:36,39). His arrest is necessary "that the scriptures might be fulfilled" (14:50). Such emphasis on obedience in the above texts tells Mark's audience that Jesus voluntarily took death upon himself in obedience to God, the essential element in sacrifice. The audience might well recall from scripture the all-important annual sacrifice in which the priest drew aside the veil to sprinkle blood on the holy of holies for the forgiveness of sin (Lev 16). If they did recall this, they would probably think of Jesus' death as a sacrifice tearing or opening up the veil to bring about forgiveness to others, especially the centurion. Later, the author of Hebrews will make this definite connection (9:11-15).

A second factor would be the familiar parallels to Jesus' death in biblical and extrabiblical Jewish literature. The martyrdom and death of the mother of the seven brothers in 2 Maccabees 7 is described as a means of bringing mercy and forgiveness to all the people. The last brother says before his death,

> I, like my brothers, give up body and life for the laws of our fathers, appealing to God to show mercy soon to our nation and by afflictions and plagues to make you confess that he alone is God, and through me and my brothers to bring to an end the wrath of the Almighty which has justly fallen on our whole nation. (7:37-38)

S. Johnson has shown how Fourth Maccabees has developed this story: the death of the brothers and their mother has resulted in miracles as well as God's blessings and mercy; even the Greek tyrant is overcome and the land is purified; "through the blood of those devoted ones and their death as an expiation (*hilastērion*), divine Providence preserved Israel that previously had been afflicted" (17:21). Similar texts are also found in 6:27-29; 7:4; 8:15; 9:30; 11:24f; 18:4. While we do not know if these texts had any literary influence on Mark, they do portray ways of thinking that would be current in Jewish Hellenistic circles.

A third factor in understanding a causative effect of Jesus' death on the centurion's confession is found in the language and concepts of Mark's gospel. These would strike familiar chords for the Greek and Roman world. M. Hengel has assembled literary evidence showing Roman and Greek views of heroes whose death brings benefits, help and even atonement to their friends, their nation and others. Hengel concludes as follows:

> The atoning death of the Son of God and reconcili-

ation came about in the face of the imminent judgment
of the world. All this was said in language and con-
ceptuality which was not essentially strange to the men
of the Greek and Roman world. When fundamental
difficulties in understanding arise, they are felt not by
the audience of ancient times, Jewish or Gentile, but
by us, the men of today. (p. 32)

The Intended Participatory Effect of
Jesus' Death Scene for Mark's Audience

From what we have seen so far, the audience would perceive
the causative connection (through obedience to God) between
Jesus' death, the splitting of the temple veil and the climactic
confession of the Roman centurion. What effect would this have
on the audience in view of their own situation? To answer this
we would need to know that situation and the problems that the
Markan community faced at that time. First of all they seem to be
a predominately Gentile community: Mark has to explain Jewish
customs and beliefs (7:3-4; 12:18; 14:12; 15:42) as well as translate
Aramaic words and phrases (3:17; 5:41; 7:11,34; 15:22,34). As
regards the problems they faced, two of these, both interconnected, are of immediate concern for our study: the intense persecution faced by Christians at this time and the recent destruction of
the Temple in 70 A.D.

The atmosphere of intense persecution is well documented in
Mark's gospel. Van Irsel has described this by distinguishing two
groups of texts. First, there are the texts with actual linguistic
references to persecution. For example, the parable of the seed
describes those "who have no root in themselves, but endure for
a while; then, when tribulation or *persecution* arises on account
of the word, immediately they fall away" (4:17). Again, there is
Jesus' response to Peter's question regarding those who have left
home or family in order to follow him. They will receive a hun-
dredfold along with *persecutions* (10:30). Also, Jesus promises
the sons of Zebedee that they will drink his cup and be baptized

with the same baptism that he is to undergo (10:39). Finally, there are specific references in 13:9-13 to hatred, being delivered up to councils, beaten in synagogues, standing before governors and kings, and betrayal by family members. This persecution is predominantly from Gentiles since it is specifically mentioned that it will be a witness to governors and kings followed by a preaching of the gospel to all the nations (13:10).

The second textual group comprises those that receive added significance when they are read in the context of an oppressed and persecuted community. These are, for example, blasphemy against the holy Spirit in attributing the good works of Jesus or his disciples to the devil (3:28-30); the storm at sea, with Jesus asleep while his disciples are in danger of death (4:35-41); the call to take up the cross and follow Jesus; losing one's life in order to save it; the result of shame to confess Jesus before others (8:34-38).

In addition, R. H. Smith has suggested that Jesus' last words are the climactic point for a suffering community: they had been persecuted in the sixties under Nero; during the Jewish war with Rome and after, this persecution was renewed with greater intensity due to Roman confusion between Christians and Jews. Consequently, believers could feel that Jesus' last words were their own and likewise exclaim, "My God, my God, why have you foresaken me?" The resulting outcome of Jesus' death in the "conversion" of the Gentile centurion and the effect on the Jewish Joseph of Arimathea could give them hope that their death also could bring grace to others. The blood of Roman martyrs like that of Jesus could be the seed of the church.

The second interconnected problem for Mark's audience is the destruction of the Temple and the outcome of the Jewish war with Rome. Some Christian prophets seem to have taught that this great act of God was an immediate prelude to a return of Christ in power, a return already heralded by the mighty acts of Christ within his followers through signs and wonders. Mark has Jesus warn against them with words like these, "Many will come in my name, saying, 'I am he,' and lead many astray" (13:6). Also, "Then if anyone says to you, 'Look here is the Christ!' or 'Look, there he is!' do not believe it. False Christs and false prophets will arise and show signs and wonders, to lead astray, if possible, the elect" (13:22).

The powerful images of Christ presented by these prophets would indeed have been a deceptive comfort to a community under intense persecution. This is why Mark has Jesus carefully counteract their message as he sees the whole future from his place on Mt. Olives opposite the Temple (13:3). Jesus warns the community in advance so they will not be deceived: "Take heed, I have told you all things beforehand" (13:23). While these prophets made definite predictions about the imminent return of the Lord, Jesus informs the audience, "Of that day or that hour no one knows, not even the angels in heaven, nor the Son, but only the Father" (13:32).

In contrast to the local event of Jerusalem's destruction, the coming judgment and return of Jesus will have universal effects: the Son of Man will come in the clouds in great power and send his messengers to gather his elect from the four winds, from the ends of the earth to the ends of heaven (13:26-27). In this universal picture, the witness of the faithful has a very important place: they will stand before governors and kings for Jesus' sake to bear witness to them, *eis martyrion autois*. Then "the gospel must first be preached to all nations" (13:10). Christians will be brought to trial and handed over to death even by family members (13:11-12). Thus we discover a new meaning for the suffering of believers: it will make possible the necessary witness to the Gentiles, and the preaching of the gospel to the nations that must take place before Jesus' return.

Nothing less than a total response can be given to this challenge: a response even as far as death: "The one who endures to the end will be saved" (13:13). This response with all of one's life has already been hinted by Mark's introduction to Jesus' last discourse through the story of the widow's mite. As V. K. Robbins has pointed out, Jesus praises the poor widow because she has given *everything* she had, her whole life (12:44). The effect of all this is that the suffering of believers is changed into a positive achievement in preaching the gospel to all the nations.

If the audience also thought that the return of Jesus would take place in a relatively short time, this also would strengthen their resolve to give their lives rather than think in terms of long term solutions or witness. It would be beyond our scope to go into this question, or discuss the texts that on face value seem to envision a limited time (9:1; 13:30). Yet the fact that Matthew finds the delay of the parousia a problem (24:48; 25:5,19) seems to indicate that Jesus had been expected to return in the near future.

In view of the above atmosphere in Mark's audience, how did the author wish them to respond to the story of Jesus death? At this point, a hypothesis at least could be suggested as follows: As a model for persecuted Christians, in obedience to God, Jesus was arrested, put on trial and confessed who he was before the high priest. As a result he was condemned to death and crucified by Roman authority. He persevered until death even though abandoned by friends, disciples and even apparently by God. He died with a confident loud cry as a hero. As a result of this obedient death, forgiveness and conversion came to a Roman centurion and the grace to make the confession of faith that Jesus was son of God. Likewise the believer who obeys Jesus' command to follow him as far as death will be the necessary witness to the Gentiles as well as the cause of their conversion. Thus they will make possible the necessary condition for the return of Jesus (13:10).

In proving a hypothesis, we usually follow the laws of logic and science. However, in a dramatic narrative such as Mark, "proofs" are not presented in the same way. Instead, the laws of rhetoric and oral persuasion must be applied. These "laws" rely on repetition, comparisons, contrasts, and the total effect of a drama. This total effect relies on a gradually expanding crescendo with a climax unfolding the meaning of all the individual parts of the drama that have led up to it.

For the gospel of Mark, V. K. Robbins has presented a valuable schema for understanding the expanding dynamics of the author's dramatic narrative in view of the laws of rhetoric and oral persuasion. Robbins puts forward the Teacher/disciple cycle as the core of the gospel narrative. The initial phase lies in Mark 1:1-3:6 with its emphasis on summons and response. Jesus' first words to his disciples are: "Follow me and I will make you become fishers of human beings" (1:17). In view of our hypothesis, these first words summarize the gospel: that if Jesus' disciples follow him all the way, even to the cross, they will be able to cast out their nets out and bring other people into the kingdom.

This opening of the drama is connected to the middle and end in order to highlight the full message. Jesus' first great revelation comes through the opening of the heavens and the voice that says to him, "You are my beloved son" (1:11). This sonship is the secret of Jesus' inner identity, and also implies the obedience to the Father that goes with sonship. The end of the drama has Jesus dying as an obedient son followed by a similar opening of the heavens through the tearing of the temple veil, with the same verb *schizō* being used. Following this, the centurion confesses that Jesus is Son of God (15:39).

The middle point of the gospel likewise links the beginning and end in a dramatic way. Once more there is a voice from heaven, but this time it is addressed to Jesus' disciples: "This is my beloved Son: listen to him" (9:7). The words they are to listen to/obey are the very difficult words of discipleship even as far as the cross and death that Jesus has just announced: "Those who wish to follow me must deny themselves, take up their cross and follow me; those who would save their lives will lose them" (8:34). Consequently, the disciple/audience's way is obedience like that of Jesus; only it is obedience to God's voice through Jesus. This emphasis on obedience is central to our thesis, for we have previously stressed that the essential matter in Jesus' death was obedience to God. This obedience opened up access to God through the symbolic tearing of the Temple veil that enabled the centurion to be converted and make his Son of God confession. The voice of God at the transfiguration also confirms the note of obedience in Jesus' first words to his disciples at the beginning of the gospel when he said, "Follow me" (1:17).

The intermediate phase in the teacher/disciple cycle is found in the teaching and learning chapters 3:7 to 12:44. For our purposes, the central section of the gospel is essential with Jesus' triple prediction of his suffering, death and resurrection followed by teachings on discipleship as a participation in his own way of the cross (8:31-12:45). When Jesus first announced this, Peter began to remonstrate; in return, Jesus had to rebuke him. In addition, the importance of obedience to Jesus' difficult word about the cross is stressed by the Transfiguration voice from heaven (9:7). The parallel sequences of Jesus' way and discipleship are especially significant. In the first prediction, on Jesus' side there is suffering, death and resurrection. On the part of the disciple there is suffering (through taking up the cross) and death (losing life for his sake). However, there is no promise of immediate resurrection for disciples. Instead, the focus is on judgment at the return of Jesus: whoever is ashamed of Jesus' words now, will find that the Son of Man will be ashamed of their words in turn when he returns in glory with the angels (8:38). So the sequence is suffering, death and parousia for the disciple.

The second sequence of cross and discipleship confirms the first but in typical expanding dramatic fashion. Jesus announces that he will be delivered up to the hands of men (9:31), then die and rise again. At the end of the section, in answer to Peter's question, Jesus responds that the disciple forced to leave family or home will undergo persection in this life and receive eternal life in the age to come. Once again the sequence is suffering, death, and parousia (seemingly indicated by the age to come).

The third sequence is even more explicit. Jesus' sufferings are described more in detail: he will be delivered up to Gentiles, and will be mocked, spit upon and scourged before being killed (10:33-34). The disciples' response is exemplified by James and John who ask to sit at Jesus' right and left hand in his glory (10:35-45). Jesus tells them they must drink his cup and be baptized with his coming baptism. The reference to glory points to the parousia where the same words are used as in the first prediction. This third reference establishes a necessary link between suffering and parousia. Suffering will lead to and make possible the parousia through a very close union with the suffering and death of Jesus: the disciples must drink from the same cup as that of Jesus and be baptized with the same baptism. Voluntary suffering and death (like that of Jesus) will assure them of a place in the coming glory. This is confirmed by the closing statement of the third series: "The Son of Man also came not be be serve but to serve, and to give his life as a ransom for many" (10:45).

In the above triple section, it is not explained how the suffering of Jesus' disciples will affect the Gentile world as well. Yet we must keep in mind the world-mission orientation of the whole gospel of Mark as pointed out by D. Senior and others. In the above sections it is only hinted at through the presumed universal nature of the parousia. It also may be suggested in the concluding section statement that the Son of Man has come to give his life as a ransom for *many* (10:45). The "many" seems to indicate a more inclusive sense if we posit that the implied audience would interpret these words in light of the whole gospel.

However, more specific connections between Jesus' suffering and the whole world soon begin to appear. Mark connects the Temple cleansing with Jesus' own death by noting that this incident caused the priests and scribes to make immediate plans to destroy Jesus. Mark also highlights Jesus' intention to make the temple a "house of prayer for all the nations" (11:17). Next, the parable of the vinedressers makes the same connection. The vinedressers send away servants of the owner; finally they even reject and kill the beloved son of the owner, casting him out of the vineyard. In response, Jesus announces that the owner will return, punish the evil vinedressers and give the vineyard to others (12:9). The same link is found in the anointing at Bethany. Jesus praises the woman because "she has anointed my body beforehand for burial." He then says, "Amen I say to you, wherever the gospel is preached *in the whole world* what she has done will be told in memory of her" (14:9).

The third Markan stage according to Robbins' division is the final phase of the Teacher/disciple relationship: farewell and death in Mark 13:1 to 16:8. In his farewell Temple address in chapter 13, Jesus announces his departure and assures his disciples they will continue on by predicting the future that lies ahead for them.

The tone for Jesus' farewell address is set by what appears to be an intended literary *inclusio* (literary bracket) by the author. Preceding the discourse is the story of the poor widow who gives everything she has as a temple offering, even her whole life (12:41-42). Key link words are "poor," *ptōchē*, found twice and "all she had," *panta hosa eichen* followed by "her whole life," *holon ton bion autēs*. At the end of the temple discourse, we find the plot of the chief priests and scribes to arrest Jesus and put him to death (14:1).

In contrast, a woman at Bethany comes up to Jesus at dinner, breaks a jar of precious myrrh and pours it on his head. The link words are the *poor* 14:5,7 and *ho eschen*, "what she had." The "entire life" offering of the widow compares with Jesus' giving of his life and being anointed for death. It also parallels the Bethany woman's total response to Jesus, who now takes the place of the temple to be destroyed. Once again, union with Jesus in his suffering and death is linked with preaching the gospel to the Gentiles: "Wherever the gospel is preached in the whole world, what she has done will be told in memory of her" (14:9).

Moving to Jesus' actual farewell discourse, we find emphasized that the fate of the disciples will parallel that of the master:

> They will deliver you up to councils; and you will be beaten in synagogues; and you will stand before governors and kings for my sake, to bear testimony before them, *eis martyrion autois*. (13:9)

Here we note for the first time the parallel between master and disciples in regard to being accused by Jews and handed over to the Gentiles that was predicted of Jesus in 10:33. As in 13:9, Jesus will be brought before the council (14:55), where he will make his confession before the high priest (14:62). Following this he will be beaten and struck (14:63) as the disciple in 13:9. Then he will be brought before a governor, Pilate, exactly like his disciples in 13:9. So Jesus' witness to the Gentiles, leading to his death, will be duplicated by his disciples. Specifically, the disciples' suffering and persecution is linked to a witness to the Gentiles, *eis martyrion autois* (13:9), and to the preaching of the gospel to the Gentile world (13:10). Both the preaching and the witness of suffering go together.

To emphasize the importance of the above statements, Jesus repeats them in more detail. First, "When they bring you to trial and deliver you up do not be anxious beforehand what you are to say" (13:11). The fact that the Holy Spirit will help them answer (13:11) shows that their trial is really identified with that of Jesus. The "delivering up" in 13:9 is now specified; it will even be a matter of brother against brother, or children against their parents (13:12). Thus there will be new "Judases" like the close disciple and "brother" of Jesus who betrays him (14:10). The possible death of the disciple is mentioned for the first time in 13:12. The manner of this death will be of supreme importance: "The one who perseveres to the end will be saved" (13:13). Thus we have an explicit reference to the *manner* of their death in parallel to the manner of Jesus' death which so influenced the centurion (15:39).

This suffering and even death of the persecuted disciple as connected with a *martyrion* to the Gentiles belongs to the core of Jesus' farewell discourse in Mark 13. This is because the community is faced with the problem of prophets who are proclaiming that Jesus has already begun to return in power with statements like, "Lo here is the Christ," or "Look, there he is" and are leading many people astray (13:21-22). In contrast, Jesus announces that the real preceding signs of his return are the persection, suffering and death of his disciples resulting in a witness to the Gentiles and the preaching of the gospel to the whole world (13:9-10).

In sum, there can be no universal return of Jesus until 1) the gospel is preached to the world and 2) the persecution and even death of his disciples which provides the necessary *martyrion* to the Gentiles occurs (13:9). Consequently, the destruction of Jerusalem due to the Roman war is not an immediate precedent of the return of Jesus. This is a local act of God compared to his final return which is characterized by a universal call to all the elect from the ends of the earth (13:24-27). This implies that there will be such elect ones all over the world — a situation made possible by the world-wide preaching of the gospel (13:10).

Jesus' last supper with his disciples seals the Master's farewell address by a covenant meal between disciples and master. The eating of bread takes on a new meaning as identification with the Master (14:22). Jesus explains the shared cup of wine as effecting a sharing in his death: "the blood of the covenant which is poured out for the many" (14:24). This is similar to the sharing of Jesus' cup of suffering by James and John (10:39). We note again the theme, as in 10:45, that death in union with Jesus will bring benefits to others, "the many." This confirms the story of James and John sharing the cup of Jesus. Thus the effects of the disciple's death in union with that of Jesus are brought out even clearer.

It will not be necessary to discuss in detail the succeeding narratives of Jesus' prayer, arrest, trial and confession before the high priest and Pilate, and way of the cross. They are all part of the dramatic crescendo leading to Jesus' death, but have already been predicted. They provide the audience/disciple with a special model in Jesus as they face similar persecution, temptation, arrest, and the necessity to confess their faith before authorities.

To sum up: the whole gospel leads up in gradual dramatic crescendo for the implied audience until the death scene on the cross. The obediential death of Jesus, sealed in victory by his last cry, opens up the heavens (splits the veil) and thus brings forgiveness to the centurion and the ability to confess that Jesus is son of God. At this climactic point, the implied audience should conclude that they too, as obedient sons of God, should follow Jesus even to the utter abandonment and disgrace of the cross, thus "persevering to the end" (13:13). In this way, they can participate in the effect of Jesus' death. This effect will be the conversion of other Gentile "centurions" who will likewise confess that Jesus is son of God. In this way the disciples will contribute to the return of Jesus in triumph by making possible the missing step, the preaching of the gospel to the world that must occur before the parousia. *Sanguis martyrum, semen ecclesiae gentilis*, the blood of martyrs is the seed of the world-wide church.

Corollary for today:

The implied audience is closely linked to the real or actual audience of Mark at any point in history. Mark's gospel is not a completely time-bound document. Mark sees the parousia as dependent on the witness of persecuted Christians and the preaching of the gospel to the world. Therefore, whenever believers listen to Mark's story of Jesus' death and hold on to their beliefs and values to the extent of being willing to suffer and die for them, they are not part of a "loser theology." On the contrary, they become part of God's planned way to bring grace and conversion to others through union with the suffering and death of Jesus on the cross. Mark feels that only a witness that is willing to go as far as death is truly credible to the world.

2

Matthew

The Voice from the Fiery Mountain
And Jesus' Continued Presence

What we have written about Mark as dramatic narrative applies also to Matthew. J.D. Kingsbury has illustrated this very well in his book, *Matthew as Story*. As in Mark, the central character and hero of Matthew is Jesus. Matthew's drama also leads up to the death of Jesus and its effects. However, Jesus' last words and actions are not on the cross as in Mark. The cross in Matthew leads the way to the final commission and last words of Jesus on a Galilee mountain. This will be a key factor as we study Matthew to ascertain what effect the author intended Jesus' death to have on his audience.

For convenience, the following is Matthew's version of Jesus' death:

> Now from the sixth hour there was darkness over all the land until the ninth hour. And about the ninth hour Jesus cried with a loud voice, "Eli, Eli, lama sabachthani," that is, "My God, my God why has thou forsaken me?" And some of the bystanders hearing it said, "This man is calling Elijah." And one of them at once ran and took a sponge, filled it with vinegar, and

19

> put it on a reed, and gave it to him to drink. But the
> others said, "Wait, let us see whether Elijah will come
> to save him." And Jesus cried again with a loud voice
> and yielded up his spirit. (27:45-50)

For Matthew's presentation of Jesus' death and the events that follow, D. Senior's study is especially valuable. First, he notes that the expression "yielded up his spirit," *aphēken to pneuma*, in comparison with Mark 15:39, "he expired," *exepneusen*, is milder. It suggests that Jesus has control over the moment of his death. Thus it confirms the final and victorious loud cry of Jesus. The description of the events that follow has many Matthaean elements that direct the audience to the author's special understanding of Jesus' death:

> And behold, the curtain of the temple was torn in
> two, from top to bottom; and the earth shook, and
> the rocks were split; the tombs also were opened, and
> many bodies of the saints who had fallen asleep were
> raised, and coming out of the tombs after his resur-
> rection they went into the holy city and appeared to
> many. When the centurion and those who were with
> him, keeping watch over Jesus, saw the earthquake
> and what took place, they were filled with awe, and
> said, "Truly this was the (or a) Son of God." (27:51-
> 54)

The earthquake, the splitting of the mountain, and the opening of the tombs, as well as the resurrection appearances are a dramatic representation that Ezechiel's well-known prophecy of the dry bones coming to life (37:1-14) has been fulfilled. While the prophecy originally envisioned the return of the "dead" Israel from exile, it was commonly considered a prophecy of the last times and resurrection from the dead. Thus Matthew is telling his audience that Jesus' death has brought in these expected last times and the resurrection of the just. The above events immediately precede the statement of the centurion and others that Jesus is God's son. Thus God appears to vindicate Jesus through these remarkable events in a way that is perceived by the centurion and those with him.

A comparison to the Son of God confessions in Mark will bring out Matthew's special focus. In Mark 15:39, the centurion is inspired by *how* Jesus died: "When the centurion. . .saw that he thus breathed his last (and cried out in some mss) he said, 'Truly this man was the (or a) Son of God' " Thus, as D. Senior has pointed out, his statement is *revelatory*: the centurion is the first person in Mark to really know who Jesus is through the way he died. However, in Matthew the situation is quite different. Jesus has been recognized as son of God right from the time of his birth and baptism: the Magi come and worship the newborn child (2:11); Jesus' baptism seems to be a public manifestation: "This is my beloved son" (3:17); in contrast, Mark presents a private revelation to Jesus in the words, "You are my beloved Son" (1:11). Consequently, Matthew's purpose in the final Son of God confession is not to announce a revelation but to bring out the *quality* of sonship.

This quality is that of an obedient *son* of God right up to the moment of death. Afterward, this death is vindicated by mighty acts of God. The stage has already been set for this obedience theme right from the beginning of Jesus' career. In the desert, the devil tempts him with the words, "If you are the Son of God, command these stones to become loaves of bread" (4:4). Jesus replies, "A person does not live by bread alone, but by every word that comes out of the mouth of God." With these words, Jesus contrasts a *powerful* son of God and an obedient son who listens to the word of God. The second temptation likewise begins with the words, "If you are Son of God," followed by another temptation to presume on God to intervene with power. The third temptation closes with Jesus' response, "You shall worship the Lord your God and him only shall you serve" (4:10). These words imply absolute obedience to God in contrast to following the devil's plans to dominate the world.

The double "If you are Son of God" temptation of power has a dramatic counterpart in the scene at the cross. There the passersby mock Jesus by saying, "If you are the Son of God, come down from the cross" (27:40). The chief priests, scribes and elders join in by saying, "He trusts in God; let God not deliver him, if he desires him; for he said, 'I am the Son of God' " (27:43). Despite his desperate situation and acute suffering, Jesus does not yield to this temptation. This goes along with Matthew's repeated stress throughout his gospel on fulfillment of Scriptures as a sign of obedience to the plan of God. This shows his inner quality of a son. Of course it must be kept in mind that the word *son* or child had a much stronger obedience connotation than in the modern world.

As with Mark, Matthew's story emphasizes the results of Jesus' death in regard to the Gentile world as exemplified by the centurion. In fact, this is even made stronger by the addition of "those who were with him." All of them are filled with fear and make a *choral* confession that Jesus is the Son of God (27:54). This prepares the way for the gospel ending where Jesus directs the eleven to make disciples of all the *ethnē* (nations) who will be baptized into sonship — in the name of the Father and the Son (28:19).

A Change in Salvation History: From Exclusive to All Inclusive

In addition, Matthew highlights a decided change in the direction of salvation history. Jesus has been rejected as Son of God and mocked by official Jewish leaders at the foot of the cross. The portents that follow announce the opening of the long-awaited new age brought about by Jesus' resurrection. In chapter 28, the Jewish elders and high priests reject the testimony of the soldiers about the resurrection and direct them to tell people that Jesus' body was stolen while they were asleep (28:13). Then Matthew adds a special message for his audience: *"This story has been spread among the Jews to this day"* (28:15). This statement implies a finality in official Jewish rejection of the resurrection. In turn, it opens the way for Jesus' final gospel statement about making disciples of all the nations, Jews as well as Gentiles (28:19).

Matthew has already prepared the audience for this ending by Jesus' statement after the cure of the centurion's servant: "Many will come from the east and west and sit at table with Abraham, Isaac, and Jacob in the kingdom of heaven, while the sons of the kingdom will be thrown into the outer darkness" (8:11-12). In addition, the parable of the tenants of the vineyard closes with the words, "The kingdom of God will be taken away from you and given to a nation producing the fruit of it" (21:43). Both the above statements, in view of the gospel ending, imply that the era of God's plan for Israel *alone* has ended and has given way to a new people of God including the Gentiles *as well as* Israel.

A final point — one shared with Mark — is the stress on Jesus' death as opening up the way for all-inclusive forgiveness of sins. We saw in Mark that this was symbolized by the tearing of the Temple veil with its exclusive access to God through sprinkling of blood on the Holy of Holies by the high priest once a year. If we look at the whole passion context in Matthew, forgiveness receives additional emphasis in various ways: First, at the last supper, only in Matthew does Jesus state that his blood is for the "forgiveness of sins" (26:28). Secondly, the most shocking sins in the gospel are the betrayals of Judas and Peter which are both told in great detail. Judas repented but went to the chief priests and elders to return the money; they could do nothing for him in the way of forgiveness or help, but could only say, "What is that to us? See to it yourself" (27:4). In contrast, despite three public denials, Peter remembered Jesus' saying and went out to cry bitterly in repentance (26:75). The sharp contrast between Judas and Peter illustrates that forgiveness is not to be found within official Judaism but with Jesus. The gospel ending seals the emphasis on forgiveness by announcing a universal baptism for all the nations. Such a baptism was connected with repentance and forgiveness, if we take the parallel of John's baptism of "water for repentance" (3:11), which was preceded by confession of sins (3:6).

The Effects on Matthew's Audience

We return now to the central question of our study, the effects on Matthew's audience. What impact would the narrative of Jesus' death actually have on them? As with Mark, to answer this question, we need to know something about the problems and situation of this community. To present this we will proceed by way of contrast and comparison with Mark.

Mark's gospel was addressed primarily to a Greek non-Jewish Christian audience. This is shown by the fact that Jewish words, names, and customs must be explained; Mark appeals to a saying of Jesus to teach that Jewish laws of table fellowship no longer apply (7:19). In contrast, the gospel of Matthew does not need to explain Jewish dress, customs, laws and expressions. Matthew's Sermon on the Mount seems to presume that the audience is still observing the Jewish Torah. Jesus tells them that he has not come to do away with the Law, but to bring a further degree of perfection in regard to its inner spirit (5:17-20). For these and other reasons, W. D. Davies and others have suggested that the Matthaean community was a largely Jewish-Christian community in dialogue and confrontation with official Judaism toward the end of the first century.

In Mark, the atmosphere was that of a community under severe Roman and Gentile persecution. However, Matthews's persecutions seem to come from fellow Jews rather than from Gentiles. In support of this, the principal persecution texts in Matthew Chapter 10 occur during a mission of Jesus' disciples to Jewish towns. In fact, Jesus specifically prohibits their entry into Gentile territory (10:5). Consequently this will affect Matthew's interpretation of Jesus' death for the audience/disciples. Their suffering and death will not be the principal factor in winning over Gentiles like Jesus' death in regard to the centurion. This is simply because such suffering will not be a prominent witness to Gentile persecutors.

In Mark, we find that the community addressed has broken away from Judaism to form a new, predominantly Gentile group. The rejection texts such as the conclusion to the vinedressers parable (12:8-10), the cleansing of the Temple to make a house for all the nations (11:17), and the abrogation of Jewish food laws (7:19) seem to point in this direction. However, despite similar rejection texts, Matthew's community seems to be very closely attached to Jewish ways and practices but wavering in regard to the question of authority.

This wavering or hesitation was caused by the aftermath of the Jewish War with Rome (66-71) and the resulting dilemma faced by Jewish Christians. The failure of many Christians to fight against Rome (24:15-20) meant that many Jews regarded them as traitors. This put a serious damper on the prospects of winning further Jewish converts. In addition, the Pharisees increasingly dominated Judaism so that their leadership, teaching and example became the norm for most Jews. This resulted in increasing friction with Jewish Christians who no longer felt themselves welcome in Jewish synagogues and society. Jerusalem and Pharisaic leadership had been authoritative for Jewish Christians until the destruction of Jerusalem and the above turn of events. Where should they now turn for leadership, authority and direction?

Their dilemma became even more acute because of the dwindling number of Jewish converts. This gradually reduced Jewish Christians to a small minority within largely Gentile communities. These latter did not appreciate the total dedication of their Jewish confreres to the Torah and traditional practices. Many Jewish Christians were faced with the following choices: 1) to return to their former Pharisee teachers; 2) to go off and establish independent purely Jewish-Christian communities; 3) to follow Matthew's advice to accept new authoritative teachers and adopt God's plan for an increasingly Gentile apostolate.

In view of this community situation, as we did in Mark, we can now suggest a hypothesis regarding the effect Matthew intended Jesus' death to have on his implied audience. First of all, they should grasp the significance of Jesus' obedience as a fundamental constituent of his title as Son of God. It was this obedience that caused the great portents of the earthquake and opening of the tombs signifying the new age characterized by resurrection of the dead through that of Jesus. This in turn prompted the conversion of the Gentiles (centurion and others).

Following Jesus' example, the audience's obedience and participation could likewise have the same effect in promoting the necessary preaching of the gospel to the Gentiles that was so necessary before the parousia (24:14). The *how* of this obedience is taught in Jesus' last words in which he hands over to his disciples his teachings with the directive that these teachings be the means to make disciples of all the nations (28:16-20). The accompanying guarantee of Jesus' presence, power and authority would make this seemingly impossible task a reality.

For those wavering Jewish Christians in the audience, other details in Jesus' death would be extremely important also. They would surely understand how Matthew emphasized the complete and absolute forgiveness afforded by Jesus' death. Jewish exclusiveness was ended through the symbolic tearing of the Temple veil. The way of forgiveness was now opened to all people, even the very Gentiles who crucified Jesus and had mocked him. In addition, the audience would perceive that the necessary witness was the death *and* resurrection of Jesus. This witness was rejected by official Judaism which spread false explanations of Jesus' empty tomb up until the very day the audience listened to the gospel (28:15). This means that wavering Jewish Christians simply cannot go back to a Judaism that does not accept the resurrection.

Consequently, we can observe the sharp distinction between Mark and Matthew. For Mark, obedience means following Jesus as far as the cross and death as a means to convert the Gentiles. In Matthew, obedience signifies the proclamation of the resurrection and the acceptance of Jesus' teachings as a new covenant to be brought to the whole world with all the authority and presence of God in Jesus.

If our hypothesis is to be proven true (as stated with Mark) we cannot prove our way through the ordinary rules of logic. As a piece of narrative drama, the whole gospel of Matthew must move toward these conclusions in dramatic fashion using the rules of rhetorical persuasion. These rely on a gradual crescendo, structural hints and repetition until the whole gospel is summed up in the closing scenes. To help "prove" the above hypothesis, contrasts and comparisons between Mark and Matthew will be helpful.

Matthew's Dramatic Preparation for Jesus' Death

Matthew uses the most powerful images in his audience's imagination in order to persuade them. With their strong formation in the Hebrew Scriptures, these were the biblical events most deeply engraved on their memories. Among the most vivid of these was the flaming, earthquake-shaken mountain of Sinai. There God revealed his name to Moses from a burning bush and promised to lead his people out of Egypt so they could return to that same mountain for worship (Exod 3:1-12). God fulfilled this promise and gave his ten commandments to his people from a Sinai mountain shaking with thunder, earthquakes and burning with fire (Exod 19:16 -20:20).

It is surely no accident that principal scenes in Matthew's gospel take place on a mountain: at the temptation of Jesus, the devil takes him to a high mountain; on a mountain, Jesus like Moses gives his disciples his new Law, the Sermon on the Mount (chaps 5 to 7); Moses and Elijah are present with Jesus on a mountain top where he is transfigured before his disciples, and a thunderous voice tells them to listen to (obey) Jesus (17:1-8); Jesus gives his farewell address to his disciples on the Mount of Olives (24:1); he makes his final decision to hand himself over to Judas for arrest at the same location (26:30). Finally, the gospel is concluded on a mountain where Jesus commissions his disciples to go out to the world with his teachings and promises he will always be with them.

For Matthew's audience *the* mountain in their memories is the mountain of Sinai. This mountain is found some fifty times in the book of Exodus as the great place of revelation and bestowal of the decalogue. The powerful image of God's voice from a flaming mountain is repeated again and again, some ten times in Deuteronomy alone. In addition, the parallels between Jesus and Moses are prominent in Matthew's gospel. This would add to the power of the image, since Moses on the mountain was God's intermediary in bringing the Law to the people. From a literary standpoint, T. Donaldson has shown that Matthew's gospel is framed about the recurring mountain scenes. However, he minimizes the Sinai motif, which I believe to be essential; I will try to illustrate this as we proceed.

With the prominence of the mountain image as a "stage setting" for Matthew, we will outline how the whole gospel leads up to the meaning of Jesus' death. The first two chapters have striking parallels to Jesus as a new Moses: the corresponding tales of the unusual births of each, the attempts to kill each child, the flights into Egypt and the corresponding return are familiar even to the untrained reader. Even verbal correspondences are present, such as the command to return to Israel because those who sought the child's life are dead (2:20; cf Exod 4:19).

The infancy stories really summarize the whole gospel and prepare for its ending. Thus Jesus' name at circumcision is given because it signifies that he will save the people from their sins (1:21). This parallels the concluding death scene with its emphasis on forgiveness. The name Emmanuel, "God is with us," parallels the call of Moses where God promises, "I will be with you" (a play on the revelation of the divine name on this occasion) in order to lead the people out of Egypt. The "I will be with you" also occurs in the last words of the gospel when Jesus repeats the same words to his disciples, assuring them of the divine presence in their mission to bring his teachings to the world.

As in Mark, the baptismal voice pronouncing him God's son emphasizes Jesus' role as obedient son right from the beginning. As an audience cue, it is meant to prepare the listeners for the death of Jesus when the centurion and others proclaim, "Truly this was the Son of God" (27:54). The audience thus receives hints about what is later to come. However, the precise meaning of *son* emerges in Jesus' dramatic confrontation with Satan that follows his baptism. There, Satan twice challenges Jesus with the words, "If you are Son of God" (4:6,7) and tempts him to assume the role of a Son of God characterized by power. In discussing the death of Jesus in Mark, we have seen the obedience theme in Jesus' opening temptation as parallel to his obedience on the cross.

Since Jesus' temptation is the first mountain scene in Matthew, it forms a striking parallel to the final mountain scene in Matthew 28:16-20. However, to discover its full significance, we must describe the Sinai mountain atmosphere which Matthew has in mind for his audience. I would suggest that this is found first of all in Moses' call in Exodus 3:1-12.

The above Exodus verses describe how Moses, in exile from Egypt, was in the Sinai peninsula leading his flocks through the *desert* as in Jesus' temptation and came near to "Horeb (Sinai) the mountain of God" (3:1). There he noticed the strange sight of a burning bush that was not being consumed by the fire. God spoke to him from the fire and identified himself as the God of his fathers who decided to intervene to save his suffering people in Egypt. He announced he would send Moses to Pharoah to lead his people out of that land. Moses however protested, "Who am I that I should go to Pharoah and bring the sons of Israel out of Egypt?" God however replied,

> I will be with you. This will be a sign that I have sent
> you: When you bring forth the people from Egypt, you

shall serve God on this mountain. (3:12)

We can note already some of the parallels to Jesus' temptation scene. In both cases it takes place in the *desert* (Exod 3:1; Matt 4:1). Next, the conclusion of Jesus' temptation takes place on a mountain, just as Moses was by Mt. Sinai. In addition both scenes are the occasion of temptation, for Moses hesitates and questions God. In both stories there is the essential matter of worship on the mountain. Jesus answers the devil with the words, "The Lord your God you shall worship and him only shall you serve" (4:10).

The sign God gives Moses — that he and the people will return to worship on the mountain — is fulfilled in a dramatic way: God leads the return to the holy mountain of Sinai by going before them as the people left Egypt: "The LORD walked before their face by day in a cloud pillar to lead the way, and by night in a fire column to give them light" (13:21). When they arrived at the foot of Mt. Sinai, "Moses came and called the elders of the people, and put before them all these words which the LORD commanded him" (19:7). Chapters 20 to 30 contain the covenant in God's own words. This is then sealed by solemn worship to confirm the covenant with blood. God tells Moses, Aaron and other leaders to come up on the mountain while the people worship from afar (24:1). For "worship" the Greek bible uses *proskynēsousi*, the same verb found in Jesus' temptation, 4:10.

With this background, we notice the striking parallel between beginning and end in Matthew. On the temptation mountain, Jesus announces that he will only serve and worship God. At the end of the gospel, the disciples *worship* Jesus (28:17) on a mountain; they are commissioned to teach what he has commanded them (similar to Moses and the people); they are assured with a final word, "I will be with you," the same words that God had said to Moses in promising that he and the people would return to serve God on that mountain. At Jesus' temptation, he was promised dominion over all the earth if he followed the devil's plans. At the final mountain scene, Jesus receives full authority from God over heaven and earth because he has followed the plans of God which brought him to the cross and death. With the divine authority, Jesus can now send his disciples out to win over all the earth.

In view of this literary parallel, all the gospel leads to a dramatic climax at the final mountain scene. Jesus' death and the following events are the decisive actions that make it possible. Here we will outline the principal ways that the rest of the gospel prepares the way for this.

The process of leading the audience gradually to the final mountain Christophany and universal commission begins with the call of the disciples/audience with Jesus' command: "Follow me and I will make you fishers of human beings" (4:19). As Jesus pledged absolute obedience to God on the mountain of temptation, so the disciples must obey Jesus and follow him as far as the cross. Since we have already noted this emphasis on following Jesus as far as the cross in Mark, we will not need to point out parallel Matthaean passages.

Just as Moses led the people up Mt. Sinai to receive God's commandments, so also Jesus leads his disciples up a mountain in 5:1. There in his Sermon on the Mount, he provides his own words, commandments and direction of life in direct antithesis to God's words to Moses on Mt. Sinai. For example, "You have heard it was said to those of old, 'You shall not kill and whoever kills shall be liable to judgment.' But I say to you that every one who is angry with his brother shall be liable to judgment. . ." (5:21-22; see also 5:27,31,33,38,43).

Thus Jesus appears as a new Moses with new commandments that go far beyond what the Pharisees taught. In this way, Jewish Christians in the audience would find guidance for a new way that would surpass that of their former teachers. The mountain discourse ends with a literary seam: "When Jesus finished these sayings, the crowds were astonished at his teaching, for he taught them as one who had authority, and not as their scribes" (7:29).

These words confirm the authority of Jesus' words in contrast to those of Jewish leaders. The coming down from the mountain in 8:1 sets off the Sermon on the Mount as a distinct unit and summary of Jesus' teachings.

Chapters eight and nine contain a collection of ten miracles of Jesus. These confirm Jesus' authority. However, in line with Matthew's overall intention, the miracle stories have only a fraction of the Markan details. Matthew deliberately trims them to highlight Jesus' *word* and his *person*. Matthew's miracles are more like encounters with Jesus' person that bring out the power of his words. For example, the cure of the centurion's servant (8:5-13) has similar elements to the story of the centurion at Jesus' death and the outcome of the gospel. It is the authority and power of Jesus' word that the centurion trusts, for he says, "Only say the word, and my servant will be healed" (8:8). Consequently, Jesus cures even from a distance, just as Jesus' words at the end of the gospel go out to the distant world.

The concluding words in the centurion story really sum up the gospel's effect:

> Many will come from east and west, and sit at table
> with Abraham, Isaac, and Jacob in the kingdom of
> heaven, while the sons of the kingdom will be thrown
> into the outer darkness. . . . (8:11-12)

This saying foreshadows the effects of Jesus' death brought out in the final mountain concluding scene. Under Jesus' command, the disciples and audience are to make possible the final banquet composed of everyone, Jews and Gentiles. The exclusive place of Israel is at an end.

In spite of this end to the exclusive place of Israel, Matthew does relate that Jesus called his twelve Jewish disciples, gave them special powers and sent them on a mission that did *not* include Gentiles and Samaritans:

> Go nowhere among the Gentiles, and enter no town

of the Samaritans, but go rather to the lost sheep of the house of Israel. (10:5-6)

However, the mission seems to be temporary and not successful, for they will not finish going through the towns of Israel before the Son of Man comes (10:23). In addition, the apostles are not allowed to *make disciples*, like Jesus; this command comes only at the final mountain scene, where Jesus' death makes possible a community of both Jew and Gentile. In contrast to Mark, the persecution undergone by disciples in this mission comes mostly from fellow Jews, and only incidentally from Gentile rulers (10:17-18). So the Markan emphasis on suffering and death effecting the conversion of Gentiles is not prominent.

Matthew's scene of Jesus' death along with its effects has "coming attractions" for the audience all the way through the gospel. Chapters 11 and 12 carry the themes of Jesus' preaching, rejection and the movement of the gospel to others. Jesus' healing on the Sabbath culminates with the Pharisees taking counsel to destroy him (12:14). Mark has "Pharisees and Herodians" (3:6) so it seems Matthew is emphasizing Pharisee opposition in view of an audience that needs to know that their former teachers were hardly in sympathy with Jesus and his teaching. As customary with Matthew, such hints of Jesus' death prompt his withdrawal and a reference to the suffering servant of Isaiah who "proclaims justice to the Gentiles" (12:18). Finally Jesus' announcement of the sign of Jonah to the Pharisees (12:38-41) makes the hints more explicit. Jonah, the comic Hebrew prophet, had been forced to preach to the Gentiles and had been unwilling to accept a God who could be loving and merciful even to the Jews' enemies.

Some of Matthew's special parable collection (13:1-51) also prepare the audience for Jesus' death and its effects, where we noted that open forgiveness for all was an important element. In the parable of the weeds and the wheat (13:24-30; 36-43), God desires the evil weeds, sinners, to have nourishment and growth until the time of the harvest and judgment; in the parable of the fish-net

(13:47-60), the net embraces all kinds of fish, good and bad; the process of selection and judgment comes later. This theme of forgiveness and openness to all is contrary to the exclusivism of Pharisee teachers.

As in Mark, the Baptist's martyrdom is a foreshadow of Jesus' own. It introduces the motif of succession and the double cycle of feeding miracles, first for five thousand and then for four thousand people. The disciples will make Jesus' memory and presence continue through a bread that will be a new food to unite both Jews and Gentiles. However, in Matthew, Jesus' miracles center more on the person of Jesus as teacher and giver of bread. In contrast, Mark stresses more the bread itself. This is because Matthew wishes to contrast Jesus' bread and universal views with the separatism of Pharisee teachers. In confirmation of this the two feedings conclude with the story of the disciples in the boat who had forgotten to bring bread with them. Jesus warns them against the "leaven of the Pharisees and the Sadducees," which Matthew interprets as referring to their teachings (16:11- 12).

Within the double feeding cycle, Matthew also brings out the authority and power of Jesus' person in a way especially related to the death scene with its culminating and powerful Son of God confession. Only following Jesus' death and in the feeding miracles do we find this title given to Jesus by human beings. Matthew prepares the way for this by his favorite mountain scene with Jesus in prayer after the first multiplication of leaves. Jesus then comes down to walk on the water — a hint of his death and resurrection. Peter attempts to follow him but loses courage, sinks and cries out "Lord, save me." Jesus takes him by the hand and rescues him, bringing him into the boat. At that point "those in the boat worshiped him, saying, 'Truly you are the Son of God' " (14:33).

This first Son of God confession is a title emphasizing power and authority over the sea and the powers of death. It prepares the way for the authoritative teaching of Jesus in regard to breaking the food barriers in chapter 15 that prevent Jewish and Gentile table fellowship. Peter seems especially connected with this (15:15) since he poses the question.

The second Son of God confession (16:16) follows the second feeding and the contrast of Jesus' teaching to that of the Pharisees and Sadducees; it is also initiated by Peter. This second confession emphasizes an authority that conquers even death: "the gates of hades shall not prevail against it" (16:18). It also centers on the teaching authority of Peter and his successors (since Peter himself is no longer alive at the time of the gospel's writing): "I will give you the keys of the kingdom of heaven, and whatever you bind. . . ." (16:19-20).

Thus the two Son of God confessions anticipate the centurion's final confession after Jesus' death. They bring out the power and authority of Jesus as Son of God especially in regard to his victory over death and his teaching office.

As in Mark, Matthew has a central section with three predictions of Jesus' suffering, death and resurrection followed by three collections of Jesus' teachings on discipleship. Likewise, the difficult words of Jesus are confirmed for the disciple/audience by the dramatic *mountain* transfiguration scene where the voice from heaven enjoins them to obedience with the words, "This is my beloved Son, with whom I am well pleased; listen to him" (17:5). However, Matthew makes some modifications in view of the special nature of his death and resurrection account.

These modifications are the following in comparison to Mark: In Mark, we saw that the first parallel to the suffering, death and resurrection of the Son of Man was the persecution, death, and parousia confirmation of the earthly witness of the disciple with the words, "Whoever is ashamed of me and my words. . . ." (8:32). In contrast, Matthew only has an appeal to a final judgment: "The Son of Man is to come. . .and then he will repay every one for what they have done" (16:27). In other words, the emphasis is more on what people actually do than on the personal witness of martyrdom.

The greatest difference in the triple cycle of discipleship is the addition of an entire discourse, chapter 18 on the basic discipline and authority of the church in regard to sin and forgiveness, a matter essentially connected with Jesus' death. Contrary to Pharisaic practice, Jesus' disciples are to search for the lost and sinners like a shepherd who leaves ninety-nine sheep in the mountains to look for even one who is lost. The attitude is that of joyful finding and reconciliation (18:14).

The same attitude is applied to the continually lapsing sinner who wears out everyone's patience. He is to be forgiven not seven times but on seventy times seven occasions (18:21). Even the hardened sinner and hypocrite is to be given every possible opportunity, first by private exhortation, then by two or three witnesses, and finally by the whole church (18:15-20). The authority of the church in regard to sin and forgiveness is God's own authority: "Whatever you bind on earth shall be bound in heaven, and whatever you loose on earth shall be loosed in heaven" (18:18). The source of this authority is the presence of Jesus in community gatherings: "Wherever two or three are gathered in my name, there am I in the midst of them" (18:20).

Following the triple section on discipleship, we have Jesus' entry into Jerusalem, the cleansing of the Temple, and Jesus' conflict situations and dialogue with Jewish authorities. Matthew has sharpened these in comparison with Mark, emphasizing the part of the Pharisees. The whole section ends with a long scathing condemnation of the Pharisees in chapter 23 where their way of life and example is condemned as a model for others to follow; their opposition to Jesus' disciples fits into a long tradition of opposition to prophetic teachings. This culminates in the loss of God's Temple presence and the loss of Jesus' own presence among them (23:34-39). This last statement serves as an introduction to Jesus' last discourse and final testament to his disciples in chapters 24 to 26.

The next mountain scene and audience cue, chapters 24-25 is

the Mount of Olives where Jesus' final farewell address is given, corresponding to Mark 13. In Mark 13:9-10, we found the picture of the persecution and death of the disciple as a *martyrion* to the Gentiles so the gospel may be preached to all the nations. So the disciple is told to persevere until the end (of one's life) in 13:13. However, in Matthew this clear connection of the disciple's *martyrion* to the preaching of the gospel disappears. Instead, the words of the gospel itself are that witness: *"This gospel* of the kingdom will be preached throughout the whole world, as a testimony to all nations; and then the end will come" (24:14).

This change in emphasis from the life of the disciple to the words of the message is due to the different time perspective in the two gospels. In Mark, time is short and the parousia is anxiously awaited; the best witness is to suffer and even give your life. In Matthew, the return of Jesus has been delayed and the audience is not faced by Gentile persecution; hence the main emphasis will be on the authoritative and powerful words of Jesus which last forever.

This change to stress on Jesus' *words* is strengthened by Matthew's view that the return of Jesus has been delayed: the servant household director begins to mistreat those under him and consort with drinkers because he says to himself, "My master is delayed" (24:48). The ten virgin bridesmaids fall asleep because the "bridegroom was delayed" (25:5). In the talents parable, the master returns to settle accounts "after a long time" (25:19). In each case the the author's advice is vigilance and attention to good works. The master certainly will return but the time is uncertain and catches most people unawares (24:42-44,50; 25:13).

This urgency of good works and vigilance reaches a climax in the concluding judgment scene of 25:31-46. The scene has many surprises: Israel is not judging the nations; instead, there is a common judgment for all the world. The nations are witnesses as in the Sermon on the Mount where disciples are to be the salt of the whole earth and the light of the world; their good

works should be so apparent to others that they would glorify
God because of them (5:14-16). No one is asked at the judgment
if they are circumcised or have kept the biblical laws. Nor is there
any mention of special benefits for charismatics who "prophesy,
cast out demons, or do mighty works" (5:14-16) in Jesus' name.
Instead, we have simple examples of obedience to Jesus' word
such as feeding the hungry — "You yourselves give them to eat"
(14:16) — or giving drink to the thirsty (10:42).

Jesus' final words in the judgment scene above link with his last
gospel statements where he enjoins the disciples to see to it that
his teachings are *observed*. Response to this final command is
made possible by Jesus' obedient death and resurrection resulting
in his continual presence with his disciples (28:20).

The eschatological discourse in Chapters 24 and 25 moves to the
passion account with the literary joiner *"When Jesus had finished
all these sayings"* (26:1). Similar endings are found to the four
previous discourses (7:28; 11:1; 13:53; 19:1). However, the word
all has never been previously used. So Matthew perhaps meant
to include all the previous discourses by using the word *all*. If
this is so, the five discourses would be a compendium of Jesus'
instructions that are to be taught to all the world (28:20) after his
death.

The passion account opens with a contrast between the plot to
betray Jesus (26:3-5) and a woman's extravagant loving anoint-
ment at Bethany (26:6-13). In Mark, we noted the literary parallel between the widow who gave all she had, her life itself, and
the woman at Bethany who gave what she could (12:44; 14:8).
This totality is missing in Matthew who does not center the passion account on giving one's life for Jesus. Instead the *kalon
ergon*, good work, is emphasized (26:10). In Matthew, Jesus concludes, "Wherever this gospel is preached in the whole world,
what she has done will be told in memory of her" (26:13). Thus
the Bethany woman becomes an example of good works for the
whole world. The use of *this* gospel instead of Mark's *the* gospel

(here as well as in 24:13) may be significant. The author may be referring to his own work as *this* gospel — one that emphasizes Jesus' words and corresponding good works.

More than in Mark, Matthew's Last Supper account is overshadowed by Judas' betrayal: Jesus knows who the betrayer is and identifies him (26:25). Despite this, Jesus goes ahead with the symbolic offering of himself at the Last Supper. In this way, Matthew intimates that Jesus offers himself even for his betrayer and worst enemy. Thus Jesus puts into action his own word, "Love your enemies," found in the Sermon on the Mount (5:44). This also prepares the way for Jesus' death which benefits the Roman soldiers who had previously mocked and crucified him. Jesus' death is an act of love for sinners and even enemies.

In line with Matthew's emphasis on the person of Jesus and his words, Jesus' verbal commands both to eat the bread and drink the cup are added. Also, as previously noted, Jesus' specific words are added, "for the forgiveness of sin." This reminds the audience to look toward the death of Jesus as an occasion for the forgiveness of sins.

The scene now returns to a favorite mountain, that of Olives where Jesus' final decision in regard to his death will be made. At this point, Matthew starts preparing for the final mountain theophany by the first of three predictions or commands. Jesus announces that all will fall away and then says, "I will strike the shepherd, and the sheep of the flock will be scattered, but after I am raised up, I will go before you to Galilee" (26:31- 32). This going before into Galilee will be announced again by the angels at the empty tomb (28:7) and a third time by the risen Jesus to the women (28:10). Finally the author will note, "the eleven disciples went to Galilee, to the mountain to which Jesus had directed them" (28:16). There is no doubt that the death of Jesus opens the way to the final gospel sign, the worship and commission on the mountain, a remarkable parallel to God's sign to Moses that the people would return to Mt. Sinai to worship him.

Matthew's arrest scene has a distinctive emphasis on non-violence. In contrast to Mark, Jesus intervenes with a command to stop the disciples from their violent resistance. He says,

> Put your sword back into its place; for all who take
> the sword will perish by the sword. Do you think that
> I cannot appeal to my Father and he will at once send
> me more than twelve legions of angels? (26:52-53)

This conforms with Jesus' teaching on non-violence in face of persecution in the Sermon on the Mount: "Do not resist one who is evil. But if any one strikes you on the right cheek, turn to him the other also" (5:39). The same word for "strike" is found in the description of the slaps and insults offered to Jesus after he is accused of blasphemy in his trial before the high priest (26:67). This non-violent emphasis prepares the way for Jesus' response to the final triple temptation at the cross to make use of violent power by coming down from the cross and overcoming the Roman soldiers and his adversaries, thus showing himself to be a powerful Son of God (27:40-44). Thus Jesus' obedient death represents the ultimate in the gospel's teaching on love and non-violence. Only the humble obedience implied by the word *son* can prepare the way for his powerful title of Son of God at his resurrection.

The trial before Pilate also hints at a central Matthaean theme about the new place of the Gentiles. In Matthew's accounts, Pilate, a Roman Gentile, is so convinced of Jesus' innocence that he has a ritual washing of his hands before the crowd to disclaim responsibility (27:24; Deut 21:6-9). In contrast, the crowd incited by the Jewish leaders shout, "His blood be upon us and our children" (27:25). In addition, Pilate's wife has a dream warning her against convicting a just man (27:19). Since God was considered the author of such significant dreams, Matthew is hinting that God works through Gentiles as well as Jews. In chapter two, Matthew has already related that God sent a guiding star so the Magi could find the newborn Jesus and also warned them by a dream not to return to Herod. All this prepares the way for Jesus' death and resurrection: it is accepted by Gentiles who proclaim him Son of God, but rejected by Jewish leaders who circulate stories that Jesus' body was stolen (28:13-15).

We can now return to the effects on the audience of Jesus' death. We have been pointing out the crescendo of hints, repetitions and dramatic plot leading to the death of Jesus and its effects. These verify our original hypotheses about how Matthew intended the story of Jesus' death to affect his audience. In addition, we have found several other areas of audience impact that did not appear in our hypothesis but came to light in view of the gospel's dramatic crescendo. These are: 1) the emphasis on non-violent love in response to persecution; 2) the death of Jesus as an act of love for sinners and enemies; 3) the Son of God title is not only one of obedience and submission; it is also one of power and authority of Jesus' person and his teaching. This contrast is brought about through the paradox of the cross.

The Impact of the Death of Jesus on the Original Implied Audience

We are now at a point where we can assemble our findings and identify with a live original audience listening to Matthew's gospel in terms of the effects intended for them by the author.

First of all, a general picture: For those in the community suffering hardship and persecution, the supreme hero and model is Jesus, especially at his death. His subsequent acclamation as Son of God in authority and power came about through accepting the meaning of "Son of God" in terms of radical obedience. This obedience led him even to crucifixion and death with all its abandonment, horror and suffering. As a result, the disciples or audience can now obey Jesus as powerful Son of God in conformity with the Transfiguration voice, "This is my beloved son. . .listen to him" (17:5). The audience/disciples can also understand that Jesus' first words and command to his disciples, "Follow me," must lead them as far as the cross if they wish to be "fishers of men" (4:19).

Now for particulars: Disciples/audience must overcome the same triple temptation to use power and violence that Jesus faced on the cross. Their attitude must be to face their enemies and betrayers in the same way as Jesus who even while dying loved and forgave those who hurt him most. The way of the disciple included love of enemies as an extraordinary sign to win over their persecutors, many of whom were fellow Jews.

In regard to these Jews, there is a consistent gospel picture of the determined opposition of Jewish leaders, especially Pharisees, to Jesus' work and teaching. This opposition comes to a head in the passion account with the plot to arrest and kill Jesus. It also continues even to the foot of the cross where the chief priests, scribes and elders mock at the dying Jesus and taunt him to come down from the cross if he is the Son of God (27:41). In view of this history of opposition to Jesus, Jewish Christians must resist the temptation to return to their former leaders.

In regard to these wavering Jewish Christians, the message is clear that Jesus' death puts an end to all exclusivism. They can neither return to Judaism nor go off to have their own separate communities apart from Gentile Christians. The reason for this is the following: Jesus has broken down all exclusivism on the cross by offering complete forgiveness to all. This is symbolized by the tearing of the Temple veil and the total effects of the shedding of Jesus blood "for the forgiveness of sins" (26:28). The continued emphasis on this forgiveness comes to a climax at Jesus' death and makes possible the subsequent "conversion" and Son of God acclamation of the centurion and other Gentiles.

As another sign of the breakdown of exclusivism, Jesus' death opened up the new age of the resurrection. This was symbolized by the opening of tombs and apparitions of the risen Jesus and other saints. Official Judaism has not accepted this and has continued to spread stories that Jesus' body was stolen away by his disciples (28:12-15). This likewise means that no return to Judaism is possible. Finally, the resurrection of Jesus has given him a unique title of authority and power as Son of God. The allegiance of the Jewish Christian can no longer turn to anyone else as supreme authoritative teacher.

In view of the above factors, Matthew emphasizes more than Mark the figure of Joseph of Arimathea as a model for the Jewish audience. Only Matthew names Joseph as a "disciple of Jesus" (27:57). Joseph, in face of danger to his own life (as a follower of a crucified revolutionary) does not conceal his faith, but comes out openly to declare his allegiance to Jesus by going to Pilate and asking for the body of Jesus. Thus he would identify himself as a family member or close disciple.

The final great mountain scene in 28:16-20 is the culminating point of the whole gospel of Matthew. This is skillfully described as a final sign to audience/disciples that Jesus has fulfilled the triple promise to lead them there (26:32; 28:7,10) as a dramatic parallel to God's promise to Moses at Sinai to lead his people back to that mountain for worship as a certain sign of his call (Exod 3:12).

> Now the eleven disciples went to Galilee to the mountain to which Jesus had directed them. And when they saw him they worshiped him, but some doubted. (28:16)

The audience, especially teachers, would certainly identify with the eleven disciples. Even though they were no longer alive, their teaching office continues in others. This is because Jesus, as authoritative teacher, remains with his disciples even to the close of the age, which, we already noted, is delayed in the gospel of Matthew. The eleven worship Jesus on the mountain, just as Moses and the elders worshiped God on Mt. Sinai upon their return (Exod 24:1-2) in fulfillment of God's promise and command.

> And Jesus came and said to them, "All authority in heaven and earth has been given to me." (28:18)

Jesus now appears on the new Mt. Sinai as a new Moses with all the authority of the Son of God (Father and Son are named in the next verse). At first the typical "fireworks" theophany of Mt. Sinai seem to be missing. For example, "The Lord descended upon it in fire: and the smoke of it went up like the smoke of a kiln and the whole mountain quaked greatly" (Exod 19:18-19). However, Matthew does have these Sinai theophany images but has spread them out: the earth shakes at the death of Christ, and also to open up his tomb (27:51; 28:2); the lightning (Gk *astrapai*) of Exod 19:16 is the same word use to describe the angel at Jesus' tomb: "His appearance was like lightning, and his rainment white as snow" (28:3). Thus the fire/lightning manifestations of Sinai occur at the empty tomb. These connections with Sinai would certainly be caught by the audience. Matthew may also have in mind the triple mention of the third day in the Sinai theophany (19:11,15,16) which would parallel Jesus' own resurrection on the third day.

These signs confirm that the disciples/audience can have full confidence in the power and authority of Jesus as Son of God in regard to the new mission he is entrusting them.

> Go, therefore and make disciples of all nations, bap-
> tizing them in the name of the Father and of the Son
> and of the Holy Spirit. (28:19)

The authoritative command "Go" of the Son of God provides disciples/audience with the power and commission for a new task ahead. The command *mathēteusate*, "make disciples" has never before been given to the disciples. It is now given in regard to all nations *panta ta ethnē* to make it clear that Jesus' final intention is a joint community of Jew and Greek. No longer is any kind of exclusivism possible since the cross and resurrection have broken it down. The mention of *baptizing* puts Jew and Gentile on an equal plane. Both need forgiveness of sins, which is linked to this baptism.

> Teaching them to observe all that I have commanded

you. (28:10)

Jesus' authority as Son of God has already been linked with teaching in his words to Peter at Caesarea Philippi (16:16-19). On Mt. Sinai, God gave the decalogue and his covenant commandments to Moses; here Jesus hands over to his disciples his *new covenant* of instructions that Matthew has outlined in his five great discourses. Jesus' *blood of the covenant* at the last supper (26:28) may be linked with Jesus' instructions, but no specific connection is made. For the audience, it may have been enough to remember the parallel of Moses sprinkling blood on Mt. Sinai, then taking the book of the covenant and reading it to the people. They in turn responded with obedience: "All the Lord has spoken we will do, and we will be obedient." Moses then took the blood, sprinkled it upon the people and said, "Behold the blood of the covenant which the Lord has made with you in accordance with all these words" (24:7-8). In like manner, the *observance* of Jesus' commandments has been a continual theme through the gospel of Matthew.

I am with you always, even to the close of the age. (28:20)

These final gospel words of Jesus are an extraordinary parallel to God's words to Moses guaranteeing he would bring back the people to Mt. Sinai for worship: "I will be with you, and this shall be a sign for you. . ." (Exod 3:12). They are now God's words in Jesus forming an *inclusio* (literary bracket) with the beginning of the gospel. There it was announced that God's plan was to call the awaited Messiah " 'Emmanuel,' which means God with us" (1:23).

In view of Jesus' continual presence promised by these words, the implied audience would *hear* Jesus' words throughout the gospel as directed especially to them. Thus the hearing of Matthew's gospel would be an *experience* of Jesus' presence. Likewise, in obedience to the powerful word of the Son of God, they would feel themselves *empowered* both to keep his commands as part of their life style and courageously undertake Jesus' commission for a world-wide apostolate that would break down ethnic barriers especially between Jew and Greek. No doubt the audience would listen to this gospel again and again as an experience of Jesus' presence that would impart new energy. This energy motif is confirmed by the world-view of the Hellenistic world where grace and words would be understood in terms of energy flow. (J. Noland)

We can now sum up the differences between the dramatic approaches of Mark and Matthew relative to Jesus' death. Mark's gospel was written in the atmosphere of a Gentile-sponsored persecution of believers. This community awaited Jesus' return within a short time. The author presents Jesus' obedient and voluntary death as the supreme example of a victorious martyr who won over even a Gentile centurion to a confession of faith. In the same manner, the supreme witness of the disciple/audience is to suffer and even die as Jesus did in obedience to him. This will be the best way to win over other Gentiles and to fulfill the necessary condition for the advent of the future. In the meantime, the community suffers from the temporary absence of Jesus, except in the new meaning of ritual breaking of bread which is an anticipation of his speedy return.

In contrast, the situation and problems of Matthew's community are quite distinct. The parousia has been delayed into the indeterminate future. The community addressed suffers persecution predominantly from fellow Jews, not Gentiles. Jewish Christians are faced with the problem of an exclusivist attitude. In response, Jesus' death brings out a dual meaning of the title of Son of God. Jesus is Son of God in his obedience as far as death. But he becomes Son of God in power through his resurrection. This means that he is an authoritative teacher, like a new Moses. As such, he provides the community with instruction and guidance through his successors, the twelve, and teachers who come after them.

Jesus' death makes possible a new covenant composed of his words and commands. These provide instruction not only for Jewish Christians but for the whole world which is offered abundant forgiveness through the cross. As in Mark, the risen Jesus is present in community gathering such as the ritual breaking of bread. Matthew, however, brings out that at other times he is not absent, but present to community members every time they listen to Jesus' teachings and commands with a sincere openness and resolution to put them into practice. The faithful keeping of Jesus' word in daily life would be the best way to win over the Gentiles in the final phase of the world before the Parousia. As the audience listens to Matthew's gospel again and again, they feel new energy imparted to them to accomplish this task.

Corollary for the Modern Reader

Compared to Mark, it is much easier to move from Mathew's implied audience to the actual audience of today. Exclusivism has been a continually recurring temptation for Christians. In addition, how can they know how to respond to evil, oppression and sometimes persecution that faces them? The question of the best way to win over the world outside is not always easy to answer.

The first and the last questions about exclusivism and evangelization can perhaps be put together. Matthew concentrates more on *orthopraxis*, right action, than on *orthodoxy*, right beliefs. In Matthew's judgment scene no matters of Jewish religious practices are brought up, nor are Christian ones for that matter. In fact, Jesus reprimands those who count on specific works of power done in his name (prophecy, miracles, etc. 7:21-23). Actions that could be performed by a member of any religion anywhere in the world are named: feeding the hungry, giving drink to the thirsty, clothing the naked etc.(25:35-45). Jesus' way of life, embodied in his teachings and commands, is to be brought to the whole world through its visibility in the lives of his disciples (5:14-16). In these verses Jesus calls his disciples to be a light to the world and the salt of the earth through a life style that will so impress outsiders that they will recognize God's presence and work in them.

In reference to evil, oppression and even persecution, there is no doubt that Jesus took a public stand at the risk of his death: for example, when he cleansed the Temple, and through his last teachings in Jerusalem that resulted in the decision to arrest him (21:45-46). However, his actual arrest and death on the cross taught that non-violent response through actual love of his enemies was the ultimate way to win them over. At the heart of the Sermon of the Mount is found this ideal of unconditional love, even of enemies, as the highest form of imitation of God:

> I say to you, Love your enemies and pray for those who persecute you, so that you may be sons of your Father who is in heaven for he makes his sun rise on the evil and on the good, and sends rain on the just and on the unjust. (5:44-45)

Listening to Jesus' words imparts energy not only to the original audience of Matthew but to any audience at any period of history that believes in the continual presence of Jesus announced by his last words, "I will be with you, even till the end of the age." The power and energy of Jesus' word has largely been lost in the atmosphere of a technologically centered and fast moving modern world that emphasizes visual knowledge.

However, the constant use of the words *hear* and *listen* in this gospel leads us to believe that the author considered Jesus as speaking directly to his audience every time his book was read to them. In addition, Matthew's double reference to *this* gospel as signifying his own work has profound significance. It makes us believe that he wished Jesus' words to be repeated again and again so they could be known by memory and thus be a special source of power and energy in his audience's lives. A return to memorizing Jesus' words, especially in the Sermon on the Mount, would be an important way to experience their power and put them into practice.

3
Luke
The Cosmic Struggle
And the Kingdom as Now

Luke alone of the four gospel writers has a double feature presentation — a two volume work. This second book is the Acts of the Apostles, beginning with the notice, "In the first book, O Theophilus, I have dealt with all that Jesus began to do and teach, until the day when he was taken up. . . ." In the first book, the gospel, Luke clearly indicates his general purpose: that Theophilus may know the truth or certainty of the things about which he has been instructed (1:4).

How could such a certainty be obtained? Knowing the gospel audience was well instructed in the Old Testament Scriptures, it could only be through the knowledge that God's great plan in these writings had been fulfilled. This fulfillment must be first in Jesus in the first volume, the gospel, and then through his successors in the second volume, the Acts of the Apostles. So Luke compiles, like others, a "narrative of the things which have been fulfilled among us" (1:1). But it is a special new contribution, "an orderly account" (1:3) in view of special insights he has to offer his audience as he reflects on what others have already written based on first generation eyewitnesses (1:2).

49

Because of Luke's double feature program, unlike Matthew and Mark, Jesus' death and exaltation lie at the drama midpoint. The first volume leads toward it and the second volume begins from it. Modern biblical scholarship has shown that Luke's two volumes are a composite, unified work with close parallels and common themes throughout. As in Matthew and Mark, Jesus is the hero of the gospel, especially in his victorious death. However, his activity does not stop at his death, but continues in a new way through the activity of his holy Spirit in his successors, Stephen, Peter, Paul and others. Those people are more proximate models for third generation Christians (1. Jesus; 2. Peter and others; 3. gospel audience). In view of the two volume work, Jesus performs a double witness: first, through the Spirit working in his own life; second through the same Spirit in the lives of his apostles.

The Christ Who Could Not Even Save Himself!

If Luke's intention was to provide his audience/Theophilus with *certainty* or truth about their received teaching, there must have been some areas of possible doubts or uncertainty. What were these? Luke does not tell us directly, but gives us strong clues in his description of Jesus' death preceded by the triple temptation he faced in his dying moments. The first temptation is from the rulers of the people:

> The rulers scoffed at him, saying, "He saved others; let him save himself, if he is the Christ of God, his Chosen One!" (23:35)

The second is from the soldiers who crucified him:

> The soldiers also mocked him, coming up and offering him vinegar, and saying, "If you are the King of the Jews, save yourself!" (23:36-37)

The third is from one of the criminals crucified at his side:

> One of the criminals who were hanged railed at him, saying, "Are you not the Christ? Save yourself and

us!" (23:39)

There are common elements in all three temptations: there is the title "Christ" (from Jews) or "King" (from Gentiles). Also in all three there is mockery at the inability to save himself, and in the third case, to save others as well.

This desperate environment makes it all the more remarkable that one of the crucified ones would call on Jesus for help and be promised salvation that very day. This would indeed be a model for the audience in accepting the disgrace and ignominy of the cross as an instrument of salvation. A confirmation of this comes in the centurion's exclamation (after Jesus' death), "Surely this man was just (or innocent)" (23:47). The special place and meaning of the centurion's statement will be studied later on.

The three above temptations seem to have a special diabolical nature as a counterpart to the triple temptation by the devil after Jesus' baptism. There the temptation of Jesus is likewise to save himself, especially in regard to the third temptation situated at Jerusalem (4:1-11). The temptation on the cross forms a fitting conclusion to the Lukan statement that the devil would return (4:13). He does so by entering Judas for betrayal (22:3), in shaking Peter and the disciples (22:31), in the power of darkness at Jesus' arrest (22:53) and finally on the cross.

But why *could* not the Christ save himself? This is still a question that must be answered for the audience. There could be no question of his actual power to do so after hearing about so many miracles in the gospel, even to the extent of raising the dead (7:11-17) and saving his own life when threatened at Nazareth (4:28-30) or by Herod (14:31-33). It would be essential for the audience to realize that the death of Jesus was not a terrible disaster, a satanic victory or the just punishment of a criminal by Rome.

Since Christ's inability could not be physical, it must have been because he was unable by choice: that he chose to obey some mysterious plan of God in the Scriptures that called for such a horrible death. Only through being part of such a divine plan could it be the surprising means to save others that would turn all the world's plans upside down. Luke's audience must have experienced the mockery and scoffing of others whenever they admitted they worshiped a crucified and helpless Messiah. This is hinted at by the mockery of the Athenians when Paul spoke of a man risen from the dead (Acts 17:31-32). Earlier Christian writing had described the preaching of a crucified Christ as a folly to the Gentiles and a stumbling block to Jews (1 Cor 1:23).

An important second consideration for the audience would be the following: it must be carefully shown that Jesus was innocent of any crime deserving a death punishment by Rome. Otherwise his death could not be voluntary and a powerful force of salvation as planned only by God. It will help to clarify our presentation if we take these two considerations one at a time, beginning with the matter of God's mysterious plan for the suffering and death of his Christ. In typical dramatic fashion, Luke "proves" his point by gradually bringing out this solution through his gospel and then following up through the resurrection stories and the Acts of the Apostles.

The principal way Luke does this in his gospel is through the triple prediction of Jesus' sufferings and death, followed by instructions on discipleship. We have seen this triple schema in Matthew and Mark. However, Luke has a unique feature not found in the other gospels. In Matthew and Mark, the predictions are difficult sayings, but in Luke they are completely hidden and incapable of understanding. This is because Luke wants to show that only the Risen Christ could reveal such a startling divine plan to bring about salvation through the human failure and disgrace of the cross.

Luke's first prediction saying of Jesus is in 9:23 and very similar to Mark 8:31. Luke, however, omits Peter's objection and Jesus' reprimand. Perhaps this is because Jesus' prediction has to do with scriptures that are hidden in God's plan and could not be understood by anyone. This will be shown in Luke's version of the second prediction where Jesus adds, "Let these words sink into your ears; for the Son of man is to be delivered into the hands of men" (9:44). Luke then writes,

> But they did not understand this saying, and it was
> concealed from them, that they should not perceive
> it; and they were afraid to ask him about this saying.
> (9:45)

We note that Mark has only the words, "They did not understand this statement and were afraid to ask him" (9:32). Luke's phrase, "It was concealed from them" shows that it was God's plan to have it so hidden. The same theme is found at the end of the third Lukan prediction in 18:34, "They understood none of these things; this saying was hid from them, and they did not grasp what was said."

What were these mysterious scriptures where the hidden plan of God was kept concealed? In the gospel the only hint is found on the occasion where Jesus predicts his disciples will obtain swords and thus appear as if they were transgressors. Jesus says, the Scriptures must be fulfilled which read, "And he was reckoned with transgressors." This text is from Isaiah 53:12, part of a series of descriptions of a mysterious, just servant of God in exile who suffers and dies at the hands of others. However, his death in view of God's will becomes like a temple sacrifice that brings blessings and justification to others (53:5-13).

The central importance of the above scriptures for Luke and the early church is confirmed by their appearance in the story of Philip and the conversion of the Ethiopian official in Acts 8:26-40. This official was traveling back to Ethiopia in his chariot while reading some of the above passages, for example,

> As a sheep led to the slaughter or a lamb before its
> shearer is dumb, so he opens not his mouth. In his
> humiliation justice was denied him. Who can describe
> his generation? For his life is taken up from the earth.

(Isa 53:7-8)

Philip used these scriptures to explain to the official the message of Jesus. As a result, the official asked to be baptized. We note in the above story that only Philip, moved by the Spirit (8:29), could know the hidden meaning of the Scriptures, for he said to the official, "Do you understand what you are reading?" He replied, "How can I unless some one show me?"

In parallel to this story of Philip, only the risen Christ in the form of a mysterious stranger can explain to the Emmaus-bound disciples the meaning of the scriptures that pointed to the suffering and death of Christ. Jesus said to them,

> "Was it not necessary that the Christ should suffer these things and enter into his glory?" And beginning with Moses and all the prophets, he interpreted to them in all the scriptures the things concerning himself. (24:27)

Recalling the event later, the disciples remark, "Did not our hearts burn within us while he talked to us on the road, while he opened to us the Scriptures?" (24:32).

In order to prepare for this revelation of the Scriptures, Luke has the two men (angels?) at the tomb remind the women about Jesus' prediction of his death according to the Scriptures:.

> "Remember how he told you, while he was still in Galilee, that the Son of man must be delivered into the hands of sinful men, and be crucified, and on the third day rise?" And they remembered his words. (24:6-7)

A third reminder of the Scriptures comes during Jesus' last apparition to the eleven and others gathered together at table. Luke writes, "Then he opened their minds to understand the Scriptures, and he said to them, 'Thus it is written, that the Christ should suffer and on the third day rise from the dead'" (24:45-46).

To sum up: Luke's audience must solve the problem of a Christ who could not help himself. Luke answers that he could not help himself, although within his power, because it was contrary to a hidden divine plan to make the helpless Christ on the cross to be God's great power of salvation to others by reversing all human expectations and values.

The Acts of the Apostles confirms this key divine scriptural plan. For example, Peter on Pentecost day announces that the death of Jesus is "according to the definite plan and foreknowledge of God" (2:33). Also, he preaches in the Temple, "What God foretold by the mouths of all the prophets, that his Christ should suffer" (3:18; cf also 4:28). Paul also repeats the same teaching in the synagogues of Antioch of Pisidia and Thessalonica (13:27-29; 17:3)

This scriptural plan of God explained not only the meaning of Christ's suffering and death but the value of the same experience for the audience as well. Only a powerful divine plan could give meaning for them in time of trial and persecution. The Acts of the Apostles hints at this audience experience: Paul returns to Lystra, Iconium and Antioch, appointing successors and reminding them that "through many tribulations we must enter the kingdom of God" (14:22). This would be parallel to Jesus who only entered into the kingdom and glory through the same path: "Was it not necessary that the Christ should suffer these things and enter into his glory" (24:16).

Consequently, the Acts of the Apostles gives special attention to the sufferings, persecution and even death faced by the audience's past leaders who are a model for them in similar experiences. For example, Stephen, one of the "Seven" (Acts 6:1-6), was even seized and stoned to death. While dying, he saw the heavens opened and the Son of Man standing to receive him. His dying prayer was for forgiveness of others, "Lord, do not hold this sin against them." As a result of this prayer, Paul was converted from the church's worst enemy into its greatest missionary (7:54-60). Luke models Stephen's death on that of Jesus. Stephen is a proto-martyr, an example for those of the audience who may have to follow him. As pointed out in the gospel of Mark, their suffering and even death could be the best way to win over others.

The history of Peter and John is filled with examples of their persecution and suffering. They are thrown into prison like Jesus (4:3). They are put on trial and released after a warning not to teach in Jesus' name. Disobeying this charge, they are again imprisoned but released by an angel and begin to preach once more in the Temple (5:18-20). There they are seized and beaten. Luke records, "Then they left the presence of the council, rejoicing they were found worthy to suffer dishonor for the name" (5:41). The crescendo of official persecution goes on until King Herod imprisons and executes James the brother of John (12:1). Herod intended to kill Peter also, but he was delivered from prison by a miracle attributed to the prayers of the church (12:6-11). Finally he was forced to flee Jerusalem (12:7).

A brief outline of Paul's experience shows the same pattern of suffering and persecution. After his conversion he had to quickly leave Jerusalem to avoid being killed (9:23-30). His mission journeys seem almost a trip from one prison to another. He and his companions were driven out of Antioch of Pisidia (13:50); a group of Jews and Greeks tried to stone them at Iconium (14:5), and they had to flee the city. At Lystra, Jews from Antioch and Iconium stoned Paul and dragged him from the city, thinking he was dead (14:19). At Philippi in Greece, the crowd and magistrates attacked them, stripped them naked, beat them with rods and threw them into prison (16:22-24). Finally, during Paul's last visit to Jerusalem, he was seized in the Temple, dragged out, beaten, and nearly killed (21:31). Rescued by the Roman centurion, he was imprisoned first in Jerusalem and then in Caesarea for two years before being conducted to prison and trial at Rome.

The message of Luke to his audience is clear: their own suffering and persecution, like that of Jesus, Stephen, James, Peter, John, Paul and others is part of a divine plan to bring them into the glory of the kingdom with Jesus. It is also a chosen witness, a *martyrion*, to win others over to the faith. As we saw in Mark, Jesus' obedient death won over the centurion, symbolic of the Gentiles. In Luke, an obedient death has the same function: Stephen's death wins over Paul; the trials, imprisonment and suffering of Peter and Paul allow them to testify to the truth of the gospel before the Jewish council, the Roman governor and King Agrippa. The last words of Luke's second volume describe Paul preaching the gospel unhindered at Rome as the result of his trial and imprisonment.

The Innocence of Jesus and the Centurion's Acclamation

With the supreme importance of Jesus' innocence for Luke's audience, we would expect the death drama of Jesus to focus on this also. This is accomplished very effectively by the last person to speak before Jesus died: the criminal at his side acknowledged that he himself was being punished justly, but after observing Jesus' conduct he exclaimed, "This man has done nothing wrong" (23:41). Luke has carefully prepared the way for this statement of Jesus' innocence in the trial and hearings before both Herod and Pilate. Pilate three times affirms that Jesus is innocent (23:4, 13-15, 22), finally stating, "Why, what evil has he done? I have found in him no crime deserving death; I will therefore chastise him and let him go" (23:22). However, Pilate finally gave in to the insistent shouts and demands of the rulers and their supporters; he ordered Jesus' execution as if to please them (23:23-25).

This insistence on Jesus' innocence continues in the Acts of the Apostles. Peter tells the Temple crowds, "You denied the holy and righteous one," (3:14). The word for "righteous one" is *dikaios*, the same word used by the centurion of Jesus (23:47). Speaking to the synagogue at Antioch of Pisidia, Paul tells the Jews, "Though they could charge him with nothing deserving death, yet they asked Pilate to have him killed" (13:28). The same verdict of innocence follows the trials of early church leaders. The rulers of the people, scribes and elders arrested Peter and John but could charge them with no crime except preaching in Jesus' name and vindicating his work so that the Jewish leaders would be proved wrong in executing him (5:28). Both King Agrippa and the Roman governor Festus found Paul innocent of any crime against Rome (26:30-31).

Luke's audience could thus be certain that Jesus their founder as well as his successors have been put on trial, and endured suffering, imprisonment and death while completely innocent of any crime. Consequently, the next generation, Luke's audience, could be assured that they were suffering innocently when they received the same treatment. Jesus and those after him entered into the glory of the kingdom through such sufferings; the audience could do the same as well as provide a much needed witness of the gospel for other people throughout the world.

The final acclamation of the centurion deserves special attention as a climactic point in the death narrative, just as it was in Matthew and Mark. In Luke, just after Jesus died, we have the following:

> Now when the centurion saw what had taken place,
> he praised God, and said, "Certainly this man was
> innocent!" (23:47)

The Greek word used by the centurion is *dikaios*, meaning literally, "just." The Revised Standard translation has "innocent." This is certainly part of the meaning, for the context points to it with the emphasis on innocence in the preceding trials, and the final declaration of innocence made by the repentant crucified criminal. However, F. Matera has made a strong case that more than "innocence" is contained in the centurion's word. It implies also "justice" in the sense of doing all that God wanted. In this case, it is fulfillment of the Scriptures. The centurion used the word *dikaios* because it had a specific meaning that would include innocence but go much beyond it. Luke uses the word in his gospel of those who do what God wants of them: e.g., Zachary and Elizabeth, the parents of the Baptist (1:6); the elderly Simeon (2:25); those worthy of the resurrection (14:14); Cornelius the Roman centurion (Acts 10:22).

The context also points to such a meaning. Jesus has just died with a prayer to his Father on his lips: "Father into thy hands I commend my spirit" (23:46). Luke intends a parallel to the very first words of Jesus in the gospel which likewise express his total concern to do what his Father wants: literally, "I must be about the things of my Father" (2:49). The centurion has seen Jesus die as a faithful son, doing all that the Father wants of him. (So Mark's son of God confession by the centurion is not needed because the centurion in Luke confirms Jesus' own statement about his role as obedient son.) In addition, the fact that Jesus is quoting Scripture as he dies points to the Scriptures as the key area of this obedience.

This interpretation of "just man" would be a fitting climax of Luke's presentation of Jesus' death as fulfilling the mysterious plan of God in the Scriptures. It would also understand the centurion's response as a final indication that Jesus overcame the devil's temptation to prove by power that he was *Son of God* (3:3,9). Jesus rejected the triple last renewal of that temptation on the cross when taunted to save himself. He showed he was son of God in his last words to the Father in a sense that indicated he was truly an *obedient* Son of God following the divine Scriptural plan and not the devil's plan.

However, D. Schmidt has pointed out that the idea of innocence should also be included within the meaning of *dikaios* if we keep in mind the principal scriptures that Luke has in mind: the suffering servant of the Lord in Isaiah. This servant was perfectly innocent: "He had done no evil, nor was there deceit in his mouth" (53:9). This is why the servant is called *dikaios*, righteous or holy one, two verses further on in Isaiah 53:11. The element of innocence seems also emphasized in the Isaian scriptures quoted by Luke in the conversion story of the Ethiopian official. There the image is that of an innocent lamb being silently led to slaughter (Acts 8:32-33). Jesus' title, the "just one" (3:14; 7:52; 22:14) is rooted in the Isaian scriptures of the suffering and innocent servant of the Lord.

Corollary For a Modern Audience

Luke's paradox of a Christ that could not save himself is more acute than ever. This is because the image of a messy, disgraceful and embarrassing crucifixion has receded into the shady past. Instead, we have shiny crucifixes, beautifully adorned churches, dignified church leaders and powerful church organizations. It becomes fashionable to consign to ancient myth the diabolical temptations to power faced by Jesus in the gospels. This is especially true for Christians who find themselves settling down comfortably into secular society. It becomes too easy to adopt society norms for success and advancement: money, prestige, economic power, academic knowledge, material goods, etc. Luke's presentation of the paradox of the cross still remains a challenge for believers who want to take it seriously. If they do, they will present a real surprise to the modern world for whom they will reveal God's plan to save humanity through the weakness of the cross. The reaction of the world will prove similar to that of the Thessalonians who said of Paul and his companions, "These men who have turned the world upside down have come here too" (Acts 17:6).

If Jesus was the Jewish Messiah, Why Did the Jews Not Receive Him? The Fate of a Prophet of Peace and its Consequences

In the opening verses of his gospel, Luke announces his intention to write about the things *fulfilled* amongst his audience. We have just studied the essential scriptures and plan of God that Luke has in mind for the apparently tragic and hopeless death of Jesus. However, the burning question in the audience's mind is the following: if Jesus did fulfill the Scriptures, why did not his own people receive and recognize him as their Messiah? In fact, to the very contrary, it was Jewish leaders who handed Jesus over to Pilate the Roman governor for execution. This must have been a grave problem for "Theophilus" as he sought to understand the truth or certainty of his faith.

First of all, we have just seen that Luke definitely states that the Scriptures indicating Jesus to be the Messiah were hidden and unknown even to his close disciples, let alone to his opponents and Jewish authorities. Only the risen Christ was able to reveal them to those who had the faith to see him and listen to him. The Acts of the Apostles very clearly states that the Jewish leaders unknowingly crucified their Messiah. Peter addresses the people in the Temple as follows:

> Now brethren, I know that you acted in ignorance, as did your rulers. But what God foretold by the mouth of all the prophets, that his Christ should suffer, he thus fulfilled. (3:17)

Paul echoes the same conviction addressing the synagogue at Antioch in Pisidia:

> Those who live in Jerusalem and their rulers, because they did not recognize him nor understand the utterances of the prophets which are read every sabbath, fulfilled these by condemning him. (13:27)

Therefore, Luke must find an alternative reason for Jesus' death sentence. This will be is found in his presentation of Jesus as a rejected prophet, coming in the spirit of the prophets of old. In Luke's gospel, when Jesus asks his disciples who the people think he is, they answer, "One of the arisen prophets of old" (9:19). The disciples on the way to Emmaus after Jesus' death describe him to their fellow traveler as a "prophet mighty in deed and work" (24:19). Jesus himself stated that he had come in the spirit of the ancient prophets who were mistreated and even killed by their own people:

Therefore also the Wisdom of God said, "I will
send them prophets and apostles, some of whom they
will kill and persecute," that the blood of all the
prophets, shed from the foundation of the world, may
be required of this generation. (11:49-50)

In fact, Jesus specifically calls himself a prophet. As such he
must, like other prophets of the past, bear witness in Jerusalem
the capital city and suffer the usual rejection of a prophet. Thus,
when Jesus learns that Herod wants to kill him, he answers that
he must continue his work until this appointed time:

I must go on my way today and tomorrow and the
day following; for it cannot be that a prophet should
perish away from Jerusalem. O Jerusalem, Jerusalem,
killing the prophets and stoning those who are sent to
you! How often would I have gathered your children
together as a hen gathers her brood under her wings,
and you would not! (13:33-34)

Jesus was not a hard-nosed prophet breathing threats of
destruction; he was deeply moved to compassion by the consequences of this rejection:

When he drew near and saw the city he wept over
it, saying, "Would that even today you knew the things
that make for peace! But now they are hid from your
eyes. For the days shall come upon you, when your
enemies will cast up a bank about you and surround
you, and hem you in on every side, and dash you to
the ground, you and your children within you, and they
will not leave one stone upon another in you; because
you did not know the time of your visitation." (19:41-
44)

The vivid scene just described is a vision of Roman soldiers plundering and destroying Jerusalem, Jesus' beloved city.
"The things that make for peace" would be the acceptance of a
prophet's message of peace through repentance and change rather

than listening to false prophets, and warlike messianic leaders who provoked the war with Rome and its frightful consequences.

Luke's account of Jesus' treatment as a "prophet" during his arrest reinforces the theme of the rejected prophet:

> Now the men who were holding Jesus mocked him and beat him; they also blindfolded him and asked him, "Prophesy! Who is it that struck you?" And they spoke many other words against him, reviling him. (22:63-64)

To present the consequences of rejecting a prophet, Jesus turns into a judge during the crucifixion story. On the way to the cross he addresses the daughters of Jerusalem as such a judge:

> Daughters of Jerusalem, do not weep for me, but weep for yourselves and for your children. For behold, the days are coming when they will say, "Blessed are the barren, and the women that never-bore, and the breasts that never gave suck!" . . . For if they do this when the wood is green, what will happen when it is dry? (23:28-31)

Here once again we see the results of refusing a prophet of peace: the suffering these women will undergo as they watch their children become horrible victims of an unnecessary war.

Luke underlines the difference between a prophet of peace and a false prophet of violence and war by a double contrast between Jesus and Barabbas, who was chosen by the crowds when Pilate agreed to release a prisoner according to the custom of the feast:

> They all cried out together, "Away with this man, and release to us Barabbas" — a man who had been thrown into prison for an insurrection started in the city, and for murder. (23:18)

Finally, to sharpen the point of contrast, Luke concludes Pilate's trial by these words: "He (Pilate) released the man who had been thrown into prison for insurrection and murder, whom they asked for; but Jesus he delivered up to their will" (23:25). This point is also reiterated in the Acts of the Apostles. Peter declares to the Temple crowd, "You denied the Holy and Righteous One, and asked for a murderer to be granted to you, and killed the Author of life, whom God raised from the dead" (3:14-15). This last contrast portrays Jesus as a prophet who promotes peace and life rather than war and death.

On the cross, we find the full judgment scene as the rejected prophet turns into judge. As judge, Jesus awards the joys of the kingdom to the repentant criminal (23:43). Also Luke notes that many ordinary people went home in repentance, beating their breasts (23:48). Another decided effect is on Joseph of Arimathea, a Jewish council member prompted to risk his life by coming into the open and claiming Jesus' body from Pilate (23:50-54). However, there is no sign of regret or change in the other Jewish officials who mock and tempt Jesus even until his dying moments (23:35-36).

There are other auxiliary Lukan details that sharpen the image of the non-violent prophet of peace: at his arrest, Jesus gives his disciples no order to resist, even though they asked him, "Lord, shall we strike with the sword?" In fact, to the contrary, even though they begin an armed resistance, Jesus orders them, "No more of this!" He even touches and heals the ear of the high priest's servant who was struck by one of them (22:49, 51). On the cross, Jesus even prays for forgiveness of his enemies, "Father forgive them for they know not what they do" (23:34, in some mss). Thus Jesus puts into practice his own preaching in the Sermon on the Plain: "Love your enemies, and do good, and lend expecting nothing in return" (6:35-36).

For Luke's audience, this theme of the rejected prophet of peace was especially meaningful. This is because they believed they had a prophetic call to relay Christ's message to their own world. In light of this, what should be their response if likewise rejected?

A further example was provided for them in the Acts of the Apostles. In this book, the trial of Jesus the innocent prophet continues in the person of his successors. Here we find remarkable parallels to the trials of Jesus in those of Peter, Stephen and Paul. In each case they are found innocent and vindicated. Each event is an opportunity to provide a witness to Israel and the world as Jesus had promised in the gospel:

> Before all this they will lay their hands on you and persecute you, delivering you up to synagogues and prisons, and you will be brought before kings and governors for my name's sake. This will be a time for you to bear testimony, *martyrion*. (21:12-15; cf. 12:8-12)

Since Jesus is on trial, not they themselves, he himself will be with them to answer their accusers: "I will give you a mouth and wisdom, which none of your adversaries will be able to withstand or contradict" (21:15). With Jesus being on trial, even death is a witness of Jesus if one dies imitating this model. Thus Stephen dies forgiving and praying for his persecutors, "Lord do not hold this sin against them" (7:60). As Jesus' death won over the centurion, so Stephen's prayer and martyrdom brings about the conversion of Paul who is singled out among those who cooperated in Stephen's death (7:58; 8:1-3).

Yet how will all this help the audience to understand what a rejected prophet can possibly accomplish by being a "loser"? In the Acts of the Apostles they will find that a mixed response, especially from Israel, is typical of a prophet's performance. In the beginning, there was a large number of fervent converts at Jerusalem who entered the church and distinguished themselves by their heroic generosity and sharing with the poor (2:44-46; 6:1-6; 4:34-36). In this number, there was "a great number of priests" (6:7) as well as converts from among Pharisee leaders (15:5).

Yet later on a change took place. Paul's preaching in Acts follows a typical pattern: first there was a good core of Jewish

converts along with some Gentiles already attracted to the synagogue. Then there was a sharp reaction from the Jews because
of Paul's policy to admit Gentiles without the requirements of
circumcision and the Law (Acts 15). Finally, a large number of
Gentiles joined them as Paul gave increasingly more time to them.
This is Paul's experience at Antioch of Pisidia (13:44-50); Iconium
(14:1-6); Thessalonica (17:1-6); Corinth (18:1-11); and Ephesus
(19:9-10).

The Acts of the Apostles ends with the same summary pattern.
Paul speaks to the local Jewish leaders at Rome who visit him
in prison. As a result, "Some were convinced by what he said,
while others disbelieved" (27:24). Then Paul quotes the prophet
Isaiah who knew well the experience of a rejected prophet when
he heard God's words, "Go to this people, and say, you shall
indeed hear but never understand, and you shall indeed see but
never perceive..." (28:26; Isa 6:9-10). As a result, Paul says,
"Let it be known to you that this salvation of God has been sent
to the Gentiles; they will listen" (28:30). The concluding words
of Acts hint at his success with the note that Paul remained in
Rome two years, welcomed all who spoke to him and spoke of
the kingdom of God.

From all this, the audience would conclude that Jesus indeed
fulfilled the Scriptures as the chosen Jewish Messiah. However,
the Jewish leaders and most people did not receive him as Messiah
because they had no way to know that the Scriptures envisioned a
suffering and dying Messiah; only God could reveal this through
the Holy Spirit and the Risen Jesus. Yet, the Jews did perceive
Jesus as a prophet, and typical of the experience of history in
regard to prophets, only a chosen minority listened to his voice.
The Jewish establishment rejected his prophetic testimony and
condemned him to death. Yet Jesus the rejected prophet was
vindicated by God through his death and became not only prophet
but judge.

The same prophetic experience followed Jesus' successors in the

Acts of the Apostles. Their testimony was received by a minority of Jews, but the missing response was supplied by a surprising number of Gentiles. Thus the rejection of Jesus the prophet turned into the very means for others to enter the kingdom. All this was a model for Luke's audience and a means of *certainty* as they continued their prophetic role in the world.

Corollary for the Modern Audience

Rejection, loss and defeat is as much of a problem today as thousands of years ago. Everyone wants to be a "winner" and of course, since God is all-powerful, why should it not be so? Instead, Luke presents a "loser" theology. There are no great external successes that would impress a mass-production oriented modern society. The only hope presented is the reality of rejected prophets who can always count on a chosen dedicated minority to continue on despite the lack of a majority reception.

Yet it must not be forgotten that prophets of peace and non-violence have never been popular in their own lifetimes. A witness of this is our own Martin Luther King now honored by holidays, memorials, streets and parks in his name. Yet in his own time, he was rejected by most people. Jesus the prophet of peace has been rejected by every race, including the Jews, who should not be singled out in any way. Yet a minority that is open to the messages of such prophets has always existed. These people are the chosen leaven of a weary war-torn world that provide us hope.

Jesus' Death as Inauguration of the Kingdom of God and Midpoint between the Gospel and the Acts of the Apostles

In Luke's viewpoint, Jesus' death in the gospels makes possible his birth in a new way in the Acts of the Apostles. To show this, the author draws strong parallels between Jesus' origins and the beginnings of the church in his second volume: Jesus was born through the Spirit overshadowing Mary (1:35); the birth of the church comes about through the Spirit descending on Mary, the apostles, and others on Pentecost day (Acts 1:14; 2:1-4). All this happens through the death of Jesus which Luke understands as effecting the beginning of the kingdom of God. This view is distinct from Mark who looks forward to this kingdom at the return of Jesus at the parousia. Luke's view makes the kingdom into a very present reality.

Because of this unique viewpoint of the kingdom as now, inaugurated through Jesus' death, we must study how Luke presents this for his gospel audience. He will do this first through the death scene and then in the dramatic preparation for it in the preceding part of the gospel.

> It was about the sixth hour, and there was darkness over the whole land until the ninth hour, while the sun's light failed; and the curtain of the temple was torn in two. Then Jesus, crying with a loud voice said, "Father, into thy hands I commit my spirit!" And having said this he breathed his last. (23:44-46)

While the darkness is common to Matthew and Mark, Luke alone makes it the immediate prelude to the tearing of the Temple veil and Jesus' last words. Luke also adds the reference to the sun's eclipse or darkening. By the above arrangement, Luke appears to be explaining Jesus' death in terms of the prophet Joel who pictured the last days and great outpouring of God's Spirit as accompanied by cosmic signs such as darkness and the sun's eclipse.

This intention of Luke is confirmed by Peter's quotation of Joel immediately after the descent of the Spirit at Pentecost in Acts 2:17-21. Peter declares that the recipients of the Spirit are not drunk with wine but filled with the Spirit in accord with this prophecy:

> And in the last days it shall be, God declares, that I will pour out my Spirit upon all flesh,. . . .and I will

show wonders in the heaven above and signs on the
earth beneath,. . . .the sun shall be turned into darkness and the moon into blood, before the day of the
Lord comes, the great and manifest day. And it shall
be that whoever calls on the name of the Lord shall be
saved. (Acts 2:17-21; Joel 2: 28-32)

With this prophecy Luke brings out that the great expected
Day of the Lord begins with Jesus' death and is manifest in the
subsequent outpouring of the Spirit on Pentecost. The end result
will be the great universal opportunity for anyone to call on the
name of the Lord and be saved.

J. Neyrey has made an excellent study of the passion narrative
in Luke. In it he provides a detailed study of Luke's presentation
of the death of Jesus as the inauguration of the kingdom. For
example, the "good thief" crucified at the side of Jesus asks him,
"Jesus, remember me when you come into your kingdom." Jesus
responds, "Truly I say to you, *today* you will be with me in
Paradise" (23:42-43). These statements presume that Jesus is
about to enter his kingdom, and can promise to immediately
distribute the fruits of the kingdom to others.

This connection of Jesus' death with the kingdom is confirmed
in the Acts of the Apostles by Peter's explanation of the effects of
Jesus' death. Peter describes Jesus as enthroned in the kingdom
after his death and distributing the gift of the Spirit:

This Jesus God raised up, and of that we all are
witnesses. Being therefore exalted at the right hand of
God, and having received from the Father the promise
of the Holy Spirit, he has poured out this which you
see and hear. (2:33-34)

To prepare his audience for the full impact of Jesus' death as
the kingdom inauguration, Luke presents Jesus as the way and
model for disciples to celebrate the here-and-now aspects of the
kingdom. He can do this in anticipation, because Luke has Jesus
make the decision to die early in his gospel. This decision is

definitively made by his victory over the initial temptations of Satan. This is especially true of the last one, to expose his life to death by leaping from the Temple pinnacle and then save it. Luke then notes, "When the devil had ended every temptation he departed from him until an opportune time" (4:13). This time begins when Satan enters Judas (22:3) to betray Jesus and continues until the triple temptation at the cross (23:35-39). There Jesus ratifies the decision made during his temptation so that it continues to the moment of his death.

Consequently, Luke invites his audience to take part in the complete present nature of this kingdom right from the beginning of the gospel. In his first home-town sermon at Nazareth, Jesus reads the scriptures of Isaiah with its announcement of a great coming jubilee year of the Lord with good news for the poor, and relief from debts and oppression. Instead of the usual explanations about a brilliant future, Jesus puts down the book and declares, "*Today* this scripture has been fulfilled in your hearing" (4:21).

In light of the kingdom's immediacy, Luke omits the proclamations of Jesus and the Baptist that the kingdom is near (Matt 3:1,17; Mark 1:14). Instead, Jesus announces, "I must preach the good news of the kingdom of God" (4:43). In Matthew's Sermon on the Mount, the blessings for the poor and hungry are eschatalogical gifts (5:1-6); in Luke they are operative at present: "Blessed are you poor for yours is the kingdom of God; blessed are you that hunger *now* for you shall be satisfied" (6:20-21).

In the same vein, Jesus sends out the twelve to preach the kingdom of God and to heal (9:1); in Matthew they are instructed to preach that it is close at hand (10:5). In Luke, the disciples are a little flock already entrusted with the kingdom: "Fear not little flock, for it is your Father's pleasure to give you the kingdom." As a consequence, Jesus can tell them, "Sell your possessions and give alms" (12:32). Thus the heroic measures of the last times are transferred to the here and now, and are no longer in the future.

In like manner, the joys of the forgiven sinner are not for a future era, but are experienced here on earth as well as before the angels in heaven. The shepherd losing a hundred sheep brings it back on his shoulders with joy and calls friends, fellow shepherds and neighbors to rejoice with him (15:3-4). The same sequence of serious loss, intense search, finding and community rejoicing occurs in the parable of the lost coins, where the joy on earth is reflected in the present joy of the angels of God (15:8-10). A similar sequence is found in the parable of the lost son (15:11-32).

Other passages also reflect the present activity of the kingdom in Jesus' ministry. He announces that since the time of John, "The good news of the kingdom of God is preached, and everyone enters it violently" (16:16). When the Pharisees ask Jesus point blank when the kingdom of God is to come, he answers, "The kingdom of God is in the midst of you" (17:21). Luke presents Jesus' presence as a sign of the kingdom's activity. Jesus declares to Zaccheus, the notorious chief tax collector of Jericho, "I must stay at your house *today*" (19:9). When Zaccheus welcomes Jesus and sincerely repents, Jesus says to him, "*Today* salvation has come to this house" (19:9).

For Luke, this *now* of the kingdom does not mean that the future is eliminated. On the contrary, it makes the future a reality. So neglecting the poor man Lazarus at the gate means that the rich man will not be able to eat with him in God's future banquet with Abraham and the just (16:19-31). Luke is also very conscious that the present nature of the kingdom may be overemphasized by some. Consequently, he explains that Jesus tells the parable of the Talents because "they supposed that the kingdom was to appear immediately" (19:11). The death and resurrection of Jesus must yet take place in order to make possible the future meals in the kingdom with Jesus (22:16,18,28). It will also open up a new world-wide possibility for the gospel — that "everyone who calls on the name of the Lord shall be saved" (Acts 2:21; 4:12).

The Power of the Name

The unforgettable moment in Luke's drama of Jesus' death occurs when one of those crucified with him repents and asks, "Jesus remember me when you come into your kingdom" (23:42). Luke highlights this request because this man is the first person to directly call upon the name of Jesus in view of his death. In his second volume, Luke will indicate that the purpose of Jesus' death, resurrection and gift of the Spirit will be that "whoever calls on the name of the Lord shall be saved" (2:21). To bring out dramatic contrast and audience participation, Luke calls this crucified man a criminal, *kakourgos*, three times (23:32,38,39). while Mark and Matthew call them *lēstai*, thieves or revolutionaries (15:27; 27:38). This means that any of the audience, even in the most desperate situation and after a long life of crime can have hope and certainty. The immediate response of Jesus promising a *today* of forgiveness and happiness in Paradise (23:42) simply cannot be surpassed as an act of compassion and mercy.

The above petition sums up a theme running through Luke that any address to the person of Jesus will surely receive an affirmative answer. For this reason, Luke stresses the petitions made to Jesus beyond what he finds in his sources. In the story of the cure of Peter's mother-in-law, the disciples explicitly *petition* Jesus (4:38); the leper also makes a formal request (5:12); the father of the epileptic boy specifically asks for a cure (9:38). This emphasis goes along with Luke's special material on petitionary prayer: Jesus teaches the Lord's prayer by his own example (11:1-4); Luke alone has the humorous parable of the man waking up his friend at midnight to ask for three loaves (11:5-13) as well as the story of the widow's perseverance in demanding justice from an unjust judge (18:1-8).

After this preparation, Luke draws special attention to the power of Jesus' person during his death scene. On the cross, Jesus seems in complete mastery of the situation. He knows when he is going to die and prays a psalm confidently with his last words (23:46). As lord and judge, he dispenses the rewards of the kingdom to the repentant criminal. As a judge, even while carrying his cross to execution, he talks to the daughters of Jerusalem and foretells the consequences of the actions of those who are putting him to death (23:27-31).

As additional preparation for this view of the cross and Jesus' death, Luke presents an exalted, powerful view of Jesus' person throughout his gospel. Mark had emphasized the faith of *those healed*; Luke draws more attention to the faith and power of Jesus the *healer*. For example, as *Lord, ho kyrios*, (a favorite title of Luke) Jesus raises the only son of the widow of Naim out of pure compassion with no mention of the faith of those affected (7:11-17). Luke omits the Markan reference to the lack of faith of the father of the possessed boy along with the reason for the disciples' failure to effect a cure (9:37-43). He also leaves out the inability of Jesus to work miracles at Nazareth (4:23-27) because of their lack of faith (as in Mark 6:5).

The stress on Jesus' name and person in the death scene and throughout the gospel prepares the way for the Acts of the Apostles, where the powerful invocation of Jesus' name is the distinguishing mark of a believer. This is built on the belief that Jesus became universal Lord and Christ through his death and resurrection. So Peter states, "Let the house of Israel know assuredly that God has made both Lord and Christ this Jesus whom you crucified" (2:36). Consequently, as Lord in full power, anyone can call upon his name with perfect confidence and fulfil the prophecy of Joel, "Whoever calls on the name of the Lord shall be saved" (2:32).

There are enormous implications in attributing to Jesus the title/name of LORD. In the bible, LORD is the name pronounced as a substitute for the mysterious unutterable name YAHWEH revealed to Moses from the burning bush on Mt. Sinai (Exod 3:14). This great name and all its power has now been transferred to Jesus through his enthronement in the kingdom. Along with the name goes its awesome history in the bible. For example, in the burning, unconsumed bush it signified inexhaustible energy; in the miraculous exodus from Egypt, it meant invincible leadership and power: "And the LORD went before them by day in a pillar of cloud to lead them along the way, and by night in a pillar of fire to give them light" (Exod 13:21); on Mt. Sinai, it was the LORD who gave the people the covenant and ten commandments with a voice of thunder and rumble of earthquakes from a smoking mountain of fire (Exod 19:18-20).

The Acts of the Apostles provides ample evidence of the use and power of the great NAME. The first experience of the name for believers is in the baptismal commitment to the person of Jesus as Peter states, "Repent and be baptized every one of you in the *name* of Jesus Christ for the forgiveness of sin, and you shall receive the gift of the Holy Spirit" (2:38). At baptism, a person calls on the name of Jesus for the first time, as Paul did at his baptism after his conversion, as did others (8:16; 10:48; 19:8). This implies a deep interrelationship and binding to the person of Christ as Jesus entrusts his name (person) to the disciple. This is parallel to God's revelation and entrusting of his name to Moses, which gave him the privilege to call on that name with complete confidence. Name equals person in biblical thinking.

The importance of the NAME is such that Christians are distinguished from others as "those who call on his name" (9:14). Using the name of Jesus empowers the disciple to act in the person of Jesus and with his power. Thus Peter raises up a cripple by the Temple gate by the name of Jesus (3:3,10). Peter and John teach in Jesus' name and with the same power and authority (4:17-18). To suffer for Jesus is to suffer for the sake of his name (9:16) and is a privilege that calls for joyful rejoicing (5:41); Paul states that he is even willing to die for his name (21:13).

At the same time, there is nothing magical or automatic about the name of Jesus. This is shown through a rather humorous story in Acts 19:13-16 where seven sons of the high priest (no less!) try to cast out devils "by the Jesus whom Paul preaches." The evil spirit replied, "Jesus I know and Paul I know; but who are you?" Then Luke notes, "The man in whom the evil spirit was leaped on them, mastered all of them and overpowered them, so that they fled out of that house naked and wounded" (19:15-16). To avoid magical connotations, the essential element of faith or trust in connection with Jesus' name is mentioned: "faith in his name" (Acts 3:16).

For the audience/Theophilus the effects of Jesus' name would be an important way to demonstrate the truth of their instruction that Luke mentions in the first verses of the gospel. The powerful use of this name in Acts may evoke skepticism in a modern world. However, the Hellenistic world of that time (as noted in Matthew) readily understood grace, faith, names in terms of energy carriers in their dynamic view of the universe. Believers would consider the very name of Jesus as a source of inexhaustible energy.

A Note For Today's Audience

In a way, ancient believers felt and knew instinctively what Einstein and modern science were to bring out thousands of years later — that we do live in an energy-filled universe in which apparent mass is really filled with unbelievable amounts of atomic energy. This has given rise to our nuclear age. In the New Testament, believers considered this energy as coming from God and concentrated in the person of Christ as never before. Invoking his name brought all this energy into activity in any situation in which they felt need. There is no reason to put aside the belief of ancient Christians in the power of Jesus' name as attached to his person and identity. Trustful calling on his name is not a relic of the past but can still be a source of unlimited healing and energy for believers.

The Centurion, the Roman World and the Gospel Audience

By the time Luke was written, Christianity had become a largely Gentile phenomenon with only a small minority of Jews.

How could this "fulfill the Scriptures," as Luke had written to Theophilus? It was almost unthinkable to have a Jewish Messiah believed in by mainly non-Jews. More was needed than the theme of the rejected prophet that we have previously discussed. The acclamation of the Roman centurion at the death of Jesus had universal implications that Luke considered to be very important for his audience.

For Luke, the centurion stood for the break from Jewish exclusivism to a world outlook. We noted that the centurion in declaring Jesus to be a just man, based his testimony on Jesus' obedient death as a son, to which his last cry, "*Father* into thy hands," was a witness. This shows that Luke presents the centurion as the example of a Gentile who undergoes a real change because of Jesus' death. Thus he can be a prototype and example of the meaning of Jesus' death for the Gentile world.

Once again, Luke gradually prepares the way for his audience in dramatic fashion so they can obtain this universal orientation. At Jesus' presentation in the Temple, the prophet Simeon predicted that the child would be a "light to the Gentiles and a glory to his people Israel" (2:32). Jesus' rejection at Nazareth foreshadows the theme of the rejected prophet whose own people do not listen to him, but foreigners and strangers do as in the case of Elijah and Elisha. These prophets performed their greatest miracles for outsiders (4:25-28). The faith and generosity of another centurion in Luke 7:10 prepares the way for the centurion at the cross and the centurion Cornelius in Acts 10 who is praised as a man of prayer and liberal almsgiving.

Only Luke has a special mission for 70 disciples with a Gentile orientation, since they are directed to "eat what is set before them" (10:8). This implies that they are not to observe the Jewish food regulations that would keep them from eating with Gentiles. Jesus presents a Samaritan (regarded as a foreigner because of intermarriage) as an example of what it means to be a "neighbor" in contrast to priests and levites who pass by a wounded man

on the roadside (10:29-37). The great sign of Jesus' success will
be the sign of Jonah — the comic prophet who had to be even
swallowed by a "whale" in order to convince him to prophesy
to a Gentile city (11:30). When Jesus cured ten lepers, only
the Samaritan returned to give thanks and was praised by Jesus
(17:11-19).

From the above, it is evident that Luke leads up to the "conversion" of the centurion at Jesus' death as a symbol of its effect
on the whole world. (We have already pointed out in Mark the
connection between Jesus' death as a "sacrifice" and the change
brought about in the centurion.) Luke would also have the same
views as the Greek world in understanding how the death of a
great hero could affect others.

This unusual sequel to Jesus' death is typical of the surprises
found in the Acts of the Apostles. As Jews and patriots, Jesus'
disciples had thought the kingdom would be a Jewish monopoly.
Hence they asked him, "Lord will you at this time restore the
kingdom to Israel?" (1:6) Jesus replied that the power of the
kingdom would have an inner manifestation in the Holy Spirit
and an outer one through a world-wide apostolate:

> You shall receive power when the Holy Spirit has
> come upon you; and you shall be my witnesses in
> Jerusalem and in all Judea and Samaria and to the ends
> of the earth. (1:8)

The above verses summarize Luke's plan in the Acts of the
Apostles which traces the movement of the gospel "to the ends
of the earth" in ways that were completely unpredictable and
unexpected. Peter, John and the Twelve at first dedicated themselves almost exclusively to a Jewish apostolate — after all a Jewish Messiah should be first of all for Jews! However, the direct
intervention of the Spirit reversed the tables completely. First of
all, official Jewish persecution against the seven Greek leaders
appointed by the Twelve (Acts 6:1-6) resulted in their departure
from Jerusalem and being scattered over a wide area (8:1-12). As

a result, Philip, one of the Seven, brought the gospel to Samaria and Ethiopia (8:4-40). Some of those scattered reached as far as Antioch in Syria. There, for the first time in world history a community of both Gentile and Jewish believers was formed that were called "Christians" (11:19-26).

Meanwhile, Peter and the twelve maintained a strictly Jewish apostolate. In doing so, they carefully observed Jewish laws and customs. Just as their master Jesus, it might be said of them that none of them ever ate a ham sandwich in their life! Peter was so faithful to Jewish and biblical laws of exclusive table fellowship that only a voice from heaven in a dream repeated three times, along with a message from the Spirit, induced him to invite into his house a group of Gentiles from Cornelius and offer them food and hospitality (10:9-23). Even so, Jewish believers were utterly amazed when the gift of the Holy Spirit was poured on Gentiles as well as themselves: "All the believers from among the circumcised who came with Peter were amazed, because the gift of the Holy Spirit had been poured out even on the Gentiles" (10:45). Despite this, Peter's action was severely criticized at Jerusalem where the "circumcision party" said to him, "Why did you go to uncircumcized men and eat with them?" (11:2-3)

There is no sign, however, that the conversion of Cornelius was the beginning of a large scale Gentile apostolate by Peter and the Twelve. Cornelius and his friends may have been regarded as extraordinary exceptions. Luke has the story at this point to precede Paul's mission and to justify Paul's approach to Gentile converts through the authority of Peter.

It is the apostle Paul, the hero of Acts, who is the greatest surprise of all. He had been a fanatical Pharisee teacher who violently opposed and persecuted the new way, dragging men and women to prison and scourging them (8:1-2; 9:13-14). This man became not only a Christian but the chief missionary of the church to the Gentile world. Luke traces his journeys all around the Mediterranean world until he comes to Rome where he makes his final appeal to the Jews and turns to the Gentiles (27:23-30).

Thus Luke's audience can have increased certainty about their faith by finding that the Scriptures have been fulfilled in a way that was a complete surprise and contrast to human plans: a Jewish Messiah believed in by mainly non-Jews! Joel's prophecy (2:28-32) that anyone who calls on the name of the Lord shall be saved has indeed been fulfilled. Only the extraordinary and unexpected intervention of the Spirit made this a possibility. For Luke, the former foreign enemy the Roman centurion at the cross, is a continual sign of the extraordinary activity of the Spirit.

Corollary For Today's Audience

Luke's implicit audience can easily be extended through time. The signs of the presence of the Spirit in the Acts of the Apostles are especially those actions and happenings that break down racial and social barriers between people. The Roman centurion at the cross stands for the stranger and enemy that must be changed into guest and friend, as Josephine Ford has pointed out in her book, *My Enemy is My Guest*. Luke would consider this change an essential criteria for any community that wants to be certain it possesses the Spirit of God.

The Source and Experience of the Spirit

In the drama of Jesus' death, his entry into the kingdom and his bestowal of the Spirit are inseparably bound together in the midpoint of the two books. On Pentecost day, Peter affirms that Jesus has entered the kingdom, received the promise of the Holy Spirit (for others) and has poured it on them:

> This Jesus God raised up, and of that we all are witnesses. Being therefore exalted at the right hand of God, and having received from the Father the promise of the Holy Spirit, he has poured out this which you see and hear. (2:32-34)

We would expect the gospel narrative of Jesus' death to make the same connection, but it does not at first appear to be evident. However, I suggest that the Holy Spirit is hinted at in a way that the audience would be able to perceive: in confident control, Jesus pronounces his last words while praying, "Father, into thy hands I commit my spirit" (23:41). In these words we find the same triple mention of Father, Spirit and Jesus ("I") as in the quotation from Peter we have just cited above where Jesus receives the promise of the Holy Spirit from the Father and passes it on to others. There is a further hint in the seemingly deliberate way that Jesus dies after these words with the notice, "He breathed out his last" (*exepneusen*) as if to suggest that his death meant breathing out his spirit to his disciples. This connection of breath/spirit is also found in John's gospel in a much stronger context where the risen Jesus appears to his disciples, breathes on them and says, "Receive the Holy Spirit" (20:22).

All of Luke's gospel prepares for this climactic moment in such a clear way that it has often been called the "gospel of the Holy Spirit." Holy men and women filled with the Holy Spirit prepare the way for Jesus coming (1:15,67) and explain his mission (2:26,36). Jesus' conception is made possible by the overshadowing of the Holy Spirit (1:35). At Jesus' baptism, Luke centers his attention on the Spirit more than on the actual baptism; Jesus prays for the Spirit (3:21) just as believers assemble in prayer for ten days before the coming of the Spirit in Acts 1:12-14). As a result, Jesus returns home from the Jordan "filled with the Holy Spirit" (4:1) as an interior source of energy rather than the seemingly outer force that moves him in Mark 1:12 and Matt 4:1. In both these texts the Spirit moves or drives Jesus. In addition, Luke prefers the term *holy* Spirit, rather than just Spirit to provide a more interior transforming sense.

To emphasize the present gift of the Spirit as inaugurating the kingdom, Jesus chooses to read at Nazareth the Isaian text beginning with the words, "The Spirit of the Lord is upon me." On closing the book he announces that the Scriptures have been fulfilled on that very day (4:18-21). When the disciples return from their missionary tour, "Jesus rejoiced in the Holy Spirit" (10:21). In the Lukan version of Jesus' instruction on prayer, Jesus says, "How much more will the heavenly Father give the *Holy Spirit* to those who ask him" (11:13). In contrast, Matthew's version has the Father giving "good things" to those who ask him (11:13).

Luke's audience would be especially interested in the effect this Spirit had on Jesus' successors to whom they were indebted for their faith. In response, the Acts of the Apostles mentions the Spirit some seventy times, more than any other book in the bible. First of all, the coming of the Spirit fulfills Jesus' promise of a new baptism in contrast with John's baptism of water (1:5). It is the visible manifestation of the kingdom instead of the restoration of the earthly kingdom to Israel that even Jesus' disciples expected (Acts 1:6). The Spirit gives the *power* that was expected to accompany the kingdom (Acts 1:6-8). The Spirit comes upon the first community in the charismatic gift of tongues that represents a new inner language of communication for everyone on earth, reversing the disaster of the tower of Babel where people could no longer understand one another (2:4-11). The outpouring of the Spirit fulfills the plan of God and the prophecies, especially Joel (2:14-21).

Just as Jesus was filled with the Spirit, so is Stephen (6:3,5; 7:55), Peter (4:8) and Paul (9:17). As believers thank God for the deliverance of Peter from prison, their house is shaken by the Spirit, just as at the first Pentecost (4:31). The Spirit enables them to preach the word of God with boldness and confidence (4:31). The Spirit is especially active in the surprising moves of the gospel beyond the confines of Israel: It directs Peter to go down to welcome Cornelius and fellow Gentiles despite the prohibiting Jewish food regulations (10:19). In a second "Pentecost" the Spirit falls upon both Gentiles and Jews in Cornelius' household (10:44-47). The Spirit falls on even the hostile Samaritans after Philip's evangelization and the visit of Peter and John (8:4-17). It directs Philip to speak to and convert an Ethiopian official (8:29,39). The same Spirit prompts the community at Antioch to set aside Paul and Barnabas for a special mission in Gentile territory (13:1-3).

In other areas, the Spirit effects a third "Pentecost" among twelve followers of John the Baptist who had not become Christians (19:1-7). The decisions of church councils are guided by the Spirit's influence (15:8). Christian prophets are moved by the Spirit to predict Paul's imprisonment, persecution and suffering (20:23). The Holy Spirit guides the selection of new leaders to follow after Paul(20:28). Finally, as a climax to Acts, the Holy Spirit guides Paul even as far as to Rome. There he fulfills the Scriptures of Isaiah by his prophetic mission as some Jews listen to his teachings, and others refuse to do so (27:24-28). Thus there is full justification for extending the gospel to the Gentiles (28:28-30).

Thus the witness of the activity of the Holy Spirit in the generation of leaders following Jesus would be an impelling confirmation of the *certainty* regarding their instruction that Luke has promised Theophilus and his audience (1:3-4).

Can the Gospel Really Change Peoples' Lives? Repentance and Forgiveness

This matter must also have been an important question for Theophilus and the audience. In their hellenistic world, religion was part of culture and rarely had the connotation of a change in personal life-style. For many it meant a mystical experience, or even a form of magic. Luke tells us that this latter was a problem for many Christians. He does this in the story of the Jewish exorcists who used Jesus' name as a magic formula and consequently were bruised and beaten by the devil. As a result Luke tells us what happened when the story of this frightening event spread around Ephesus:

> Many of those who were now believers came, confessing and divulging their practices. And a number of those who practiced magic arts brought their books

together and burned them in the sight of all. (Acts
19:18-19)

In view of this environment, Luke gives great attention to the
matter of forgiveness that is accompanied by concrete change or
repentance. This is especially the case in the story of Jesus' death.
There, the remarkable change in one of the criminals crucified
with Jesus earned him an immediate place in paradise (23:39-43).
In Mark, we pointed out that the tearing of the veil pointed to
the end of Jewish exclusivism with God's access and forgiveness
open to all.

However, Luke alone notes the visible effects Jesus' death
had on many of the people present: "All the multitudes who
assembled to see the sight, when they saw what had taken place,
returned home beating their breasts" (23:48). This beating of
the breast is a gesture of repentance, the same as that of the
tax collector who went up to the Temple and prayed from a distance, "God be merciful to me a sinner" (18:13). Consequently
he returned home justified (18:14) in contrast to the Pharisee in
the same story. Likewise, Luke in his passion drama contrasts
Jesus' enemies to those who really understand what is happening.
The faithful women at the foot of the cross are also mentioned
by Luke in contrast to the disciples whom Satan desires to sift as
wheat (22:31). Joseph of Arimathea is distinguished from those of
the council who had not consented to their condemnation; indeed
he risks his life to ask from Pilate the body of Jesus (23:50-56)

In accord with dramatic sequence, the gospel narrative prepares
the way for these examples by highlighting those who make a
real change in their lives in response to Jesus' call or invitation.
When Jesus first calls Peter and his companion fishermen, Luke
writes that they "left *everything* and followed him" (5:11). This
totality becomes evident in comparison to Matthew and Mark who
mention that they left father and hired servants (Mark 1:20; Matt
4:22). When Jesus calls Levi, Luke relates that the tax collector
"left *everything* and followed him" (4:28). Not only that, Levi also

celebrated by throwing a big party to which he invited friends and fellow tax collectors (4:29).

Luke alone notes that Jesus attracted so much special attention from tax collectors and sinners that "the Pharisees and scribes murmured saying, 'This man receives sinners and eats with them'" (15:1-2). As an example of failure to respond, Luke highlights the call of the rich ruler. Jesus said to him, "One thing you still lack. Sell all that you have and distribute to the poor, and you will have treasure in heaven; and come, follow me." Luke then adds, "But when he heard this he became sad, for he was very rich" (18:22-23).

As a final example of repentance before the passion narrative, Luke presents the example of Zaccheus the notorious chief tax collector of Jericho. Luke describes him as a small man, perhaps hinting that he was small in more ways than one. On hearing Jesus was entering Jericho this small man was afraid he would not be able to see him and climbed up a tree for a better view. Jesus rewarded him for his desire to "go out on a limb" for him, and chose his home for hospitality rather than the homes of all the virtuous religious leaders. This caused great murmurings and complaints in town as they said, "He has gone in to be the guest of a man who is a sinner" (19:7). In a total response to Jesus, Zacchaeus not only stood up, but actually took a stand on his former life and said, "Behold, Lord, the half of my goods I give to the poor; and if I have defrauded any one of anything, I restore it fourfold." These were signs of a conversion that went far beyond the requirements of justice. Luke presents them as a model for gospel listeners to go all the way in following Christ.

Luke's second volume presents a convincing portrait of the remarkable effects that Jesus' death had on people's lives. Peter's first proclamation of the gospel on Pentecost day ends with the words, "Let all the house of Israel know assuredly that God has made him both Lord and Christ whom you crucified" (2:36). Luke carefully notes the response: "Now when they heard this they were cut to the heart and said to Peter and the rest of the apostles, 'Brethren, what shall we do?'" (2:37). This is the same question that the crowds address to John the Bapist after his preaching of repentance (Luke 3:10). Peter replied, "Repent and be baptized everyone of you in the name of Jesus Christ for the forgiveness of sin and you shall receive the gift of the Holy Spirit" (Acts 2:39).

This repentance took a very practical form in extraordinary generosity and sharing with the poor and hungry:.

> And all who believed were together and had all things in common; and they sold their possessions and goods and distributed them to all, as any had need. (2:45)

This generous sharing puts in practice the repentance suggested by the Baptist in the gospel: "The one with two coats should share with someone with none; the person with food should do likewise" (3:11). The selling of possessions fulfills Jesus words, "Fear not little flock. . .sell your possessions" (12:32) and similar words to the rich ruler who wanted to be a disciple of Jesus (18:22). As a part of practical repentance, this relief of the poor and hungry is not regarded as part of a distant future but is to take place now. For added emphasis, Luke notes again,

> Now the company of those believed were of one heart and soul, and no one said that any of the things they possessed were their own, but they had everything in common. . . .there was not a needy person among them, for as many as were possessors of lands or houses sold them, and brought the proceeds of what was sold and laid it at the apostles' feet; and distribution was made to each as any had need. (4:32-35)

To make this help for need most effective, the early believers in Jerusalem had a daily distribution of food and clothing for needy widows and others. The twelve themselves waited on the tables until the numbers required further assistance (6:1-5). This was to follow the model set by Jesus at the last supper, who said, "Let the greatest among you become as the youngest, and the leader as one who serves" (22:26).

This concern for the hungry went out not only to local people but to other cities and communities as well. For example, a widespread famine broke out during the reign of the Roman emperor Claudius. The Christian community at Antioch took up a collection for communities in Judea who had been especially hard hit, sending the relief through Barnabas and Paul (11:29). In addition, it seems that Luke knew about the large collection Paul made in his Greek churches for the needy and poor in Jerusalem (1 Cor 8-9). This is shown by the list of the names of Paul's companions who came to Jerusalem from many other communities (Acts 20:4). Paul refers to this in the Acts of the Apostles when he says to the Roman governor Felix that he came to Jerusalem after many years "to bring to my nation alms and offerings" (24:17).

Eating and Drinking with Jesus and the Poor

There are definite indications that Luke's audience needed more certainty about the effects of their ritual breaking of bread. Was Jesus really present with them in these meals? Was this their imaginations, or something like his ghost? Was it the same flesh and blood reality that Peter and the twelve had seen and touched? We know this was a problem from the fact that only Luke includes a post-resurrection appearance of Jesus at table where the disciples were "startled and frightened, and supposed they saw a spirit" (24:37). Jesus had to reassure them by showing his hands and feet and eating food in their presence (24:39-41). Luke's audience/Theophilus would certainly need assurance in such a matter.

The only firm basis for the reality of Jesus' continued presence with the community in the breaking of bread was in the effects of Jesus' death: the entry of Jesus into his kingdom which made it possible for others as shown by the penitent criminal who was assured he would be with Jesus in paradise on that very day. Consequently, if the community's breaking of bread ritual is to have any effect, it must be connected with the kingdom made possible by Jesus' death.

To make this connection, Luke makes careful links betweens the coming kingdom, the death of Jesus and the breaking of bread. He does this through his long last supper account which takes the literary form of a farewell discourse and succession narrative. Luke places special emphasis on the fact that this will be Jesus' last meal with them, and that he will not eat again with them until he does so in the kingdom of God:

> I have earnestly desired to eat this passover with you
> before I suffer; for I tell you I shall not eat it (again)
> until it is fulfilled in the kingdom of God. (22:14)

We note in this verse the triple connection between Jesus' suffering, eating with them again, and the kingdom of God. Only Luke mentions the kingdom four times at the last supper to make the connection between future meals and the kingdom as strong as possible. The same promise is repeated in regard to the wine cup: "I tell you that from now on I shall not drink of the fruit of the vine until the kingdom of God comes" (22:18). Then a third and fourth time:

> As my Father appointed a kingdom for me so do I
> appoint for you that you may eat and drink at my table
> in my kingdom, and sit on thrones judging the twelve
> tribes of Israel. (22:29-30)

Here we draw attention to the transfer of the kingdom from the Father to Jesus so he can say "my table and my kingdom." This kingdom now is given over and shared with the twelve so they become co-judges with Jesus. This strengthens the strong succession motif also in the future meals with Jesus. To prepare for this, it is *Peter and John* that Jesus sends to prepare the passover and last supper (22:8). It is the *apostles* who sit at table with Jesus when the hour comes (22:14).

Consequently, in describing the effects of Jesus' death in the

post-resurrection stories, Luke focuses his attention on the meals
with Jesus. He omits any appearance of the risen Jesus to the
women as in Matthew. Both apparitions are described in great
detail and take place at table: the first when Jesus reveals himself to the disciples when they break bread with the mysterious
stranger (24:30-31); the second is also at table where Jesus appears
to the eleven and others, asks for something to eat and gives his
final message to them (24:36-49).

To prepare the way for the first apparition, Luke has the two
disciples meet a stranger on the road to Emmaus. The traveler
begins to converse with them about the events just transpired and
points out the connection between the sufferings of Christ and
the kingdom: "Was it not necessary that the Christ should suffer
these things and enter into his glory?" (24:26). The "glory" refers
to the kingdom as in texts like 9:26 and 21:27, which unite the
coming of the Son of Man and the glory of the kingdom. At the
end of the conversation, the disciples came to their destination,
but the stranger appeared to be going further. They pressed him
to stay with them and accept hospitality. As a result,

> When he was at table with them, he took the bread
> and blessed, and broke it, and gave it to them. And
> their eyes were opened and they recognized him; and
> he vanished out of their sight. (24:30-31)

This revelation of Jesus' presence is a climactic point of the
gospel for Luke's audience. A look at the structure of the gospel
will show that he has been preparing the audience for this all along
by connecting the Emmaus breaking of bread with the beginning
and middle of the gospel, as well as with the last supper.

First of all, the story of Jesus' birth has the same emphasis on
bread and hospitality found at the end of the gospel:

> She gave birth to her first-born son and wrapped
> him in swaddling clothes, and laid him in a manger,
> because there was no place for them in the inn. (2:7)

The manger in this text has special meaning because Luke calls it a sign: "This shall be a sign to you: you will find a child wrapped in swaddling clothes and lying in a manger" (2:12). It is then mentioned a third time, in fulfillment, when the shepherds come and find Mary and Joseph and "the child lying in a manger" (2:16). This triple concentration on the manger invites us to look for a hidden meaning from the scriptures. C. Giblin has shown that Luke's message is woven into scriptural passages more familiar to his audience than to most modern readers. While a manger simply means an eating trough for animals, the word has a special place among the first words of the great prophet Isaiah where God announces, "The ox knows its owner, and the ass its master's *manger*, but Israel does not know, my people do not understand" (1:3).

For Isaiah, Luke, and even a modern audience, the ass has the popular reputation of being the dumbest of all animals. However, it does know where to go for its meals: to its *master's manger*. Through this scriptural allusion Luke is telling his audience that the child Jesus in a manger is a sign that he is the source of bread and nourishment for all people. It is truly the manger of the *Lord* as in Isaiah. Thus we have the theme of bread and nourishment at the beginning of the gospel to match Jesus' revelation of himself in the breaking of bread at Emmaus at the end of the gospel.

The second connecting theme between beginning and end is hospitality illustrated by the words, "There was no room for them at the inn" (2:7). This same hospitality motif is found in the two disciples' invitation to the mysterious stranger to join them at the place they were staying: "He appeared to be going further, but they constrained him, saying, 'Stay with us for it is toward the evening and the day is now far spent.' So he went in to stay with them" (24:29).

Luke's middle point connection is found in his arrangement of Jesus' multiplication of loaves for the five thousand. The setting is Jesus' withdrawal of the apostles to Bethsaida following their missionary tour: "When the crowds learned of it, they followed him; and he welcomed them and spoke to them of the kingdom of God" (9:11). The welcoming, *apodexamenos* suggests a gracious host and hospitality; this along with mention of the *apostles* (9:10) and the *kingdom of God* bring out links with the last supper and the Emmaus bread revelation.

In addition, the expression, "Now the day began to decline" (9:12) is the same as that at Emmaus (24:29) before the disciples invite the risen Jesus (in form of the mysterious stranger) to stay with them. Jesus is the generous host at the meal for the five thousand and also the same host at Emmaus who breaks bread for the disciples.

However, the most important coincidence of the two accounts lies in Jesus' action of blessing, breaking and distributing bread, which is virtually the same in both actions. We place them in parallel columns for comparison:

Luke 9:16	Luke 24:30
Taking the five loaves and the two fish	Taking the bread (loaf)
he blessed them and broke	He blessed and having broke
he continued to give to them	he continued to give to them

Luke makes the comparison specifically to the meal at Emmaus and not to the last supper where there is no mention of a blessing, but of a Greek *thanksgiving* which Jesus pronounces on both the bread and the cup. Luke does this because Jesus at the last supper emphasized that he would eat again with them only in the *kingdom of God* (22:30). Thus the breaking of bread at Emmaus is a fulfillment of this promise and a pledge for the future.

To sum up, we find that Luke has neatly connected together the beginning and end as well as the middle of the gospel in reference to the importance of this bread of Jesus. All this is made possible by Jesus' death, to which the last supper looked forward as the means to continue the presence of Jesus through meals with him once more.

The Acts of the Apostles continues this important witness of the centrality of Jesus' continued presence with his disciples in the breaking of bread. Peter tells Cornelius and his friends: "We ate and drank with him after his resurrection" (10:41). Paul also spoke to the church at Troas "on the first day of the week, when we were gathered together to break bread" (20:7). Earlier in Jerusalem, the reference to the "apostles' teaching, fellowship, breaking of bread and prayers" (2:42) seems to refer to meals with the risen Jesus, especially in view of the mention of the apostles and special prayers.

Thus we can conclude that Luke presents Jesus' death as the essential means toward providing new meals with the risen Savior. This is because Jesus' death makes it possible for him as well as others to enter into the kingdom. Thus Jesus can promise them at the last supper that they will eat and drink with him in the kingdom of God. To prepare for this central place of bread in his gospel, Luke carefully connects for his audience the beginning, middle and end of the gospel through the themes of bread and hospitality.

However, Luke is not thinking only of spiritual meals with the risen Christ. He has effectively connected these meals with hospitality for the poor and hungry. We recall that the Emmaus meal was a real meal given in hospitality for a stranger. The two disciples said to him, "Stay with us for it is toward evening and the day is now far spent" (24:29). This hospitality forms a deliberate contrast to its lack at Jesus' birth when "there was no place for them at the inn" (2:7).

The hospitality motif also links with the same theme at the loaves multiplication where Jesus the generous host provides a meal for five thousand people. Jesus' emphatic command, "You yourselves give them something to eat" (9:13) is understood in the Acts of the Apostles as a literal command that must always be obeyed. Evidence of this is found in the apostles' actually waiting on table in daily meals and distributions for the widows and the poor (Acts 6:1-6).

Luke gives so much attention to food in his gospel that his gospel might well be called the "Gospel of Bread." Even before Jesus' birth, Mary his mother sings in her Magnificat, that God is one who "fills the hungry with good things" (1:53). When the crowds ask John the Baptist what to do in repentance, he replies that those who have food should share with those who have none (3:11). In Jesus' Sermon on the Mount, he announces a present blessing for the poor and hungry: "Blessed are you that hunger now for you shall be satisfied" (6:11).

Luke's version of the Lord's prayer has a unique "twist" that links the bread petition to the daily distribution to the poor in the Acts of the Apostles. Luke has "Give us *each day* our daily bread" (11:3). This is the same expression the author uses in the Acts of the Apostles for meals *each day* for the widows and poor that were provided by generous Christians (6:1). In Luke's banquet parables the same concern for the hungry and poor is evident. For example,

> When you give a dinner or a banquet, do not invite your friends or your brothers or your kinsmen or rich neighbors, lest they also invite you in return, and you be repaid. But when you give a feast invite the poor, the maimed, the lame, the blind, and you will be blessed, because they cannot repay you. You will be repaid at the resurrection of the just. (14:12-14)

Corollary for A Modern Audience

Even more than an ancient audience, modern believers need to take seriously Luke's central vision of the death of Jesus as making possible a table of the Lord that includes the poor and hungry. Luke would not understand a ritual meal with the risen Lord that the hungry could not share. For Luke, social concerns were not an "elective" but part of the message of Jesus' death as providing for new meals with the risen Lord.

Jesus' Prayer For Others on the Cross

"Father, forgive them; for they know not what they do" (23:34).
First we must acknowledge that this verse is missing in many
prominent Greek texts, yet present in other equally important
ones. Regardless of whether it is original to Luke or not, it was
read as part of the gospel to many communities. Likewise, even if
the text is not original, Luke does have Jesus praying with the final
words, "Father, into thy hands, I commit my spirit" (23:46). Yet,
even if there were no words of prayer, the audience would have
understood the whole action of Jesus on the cross as a prayer.
What he did was in obedience to his Father and the Scriptures.
This was considered the most effective sacrifice and prayer. The
Temple sacrifices were considered as prayers because they were
done in obedience to God. So the psalmist likens his prayers
to the sacrificial offerings: "Let my prayer be counted as incense
before you, and the lifting up of my hands as an evening sacrifice"
(141:2).

The prayer, "Father forgive them" really verbalizes the whole
prayer atmosphere of the cross. It is Jesus' prayer that makes
possible the dramatic conversion of a crucified criminal even in
the last moments of his life. For Luke's audience, this prayer is
extremely important as the source as well as model for their own
confident prayers. So the author has prepared for this important
teaching as he writes the gospel drama.

The following are examples of Jesus' previous effective prayer:
at the Jordan, after his baptism, he prays for the coming of the
spirit (3:21), just as the first believers assemble in prayer to ask for
the spirit before the first Pentecost (Acts 1:14); he prays and fasts
to overcome the devil's temptation (4:1-13); before appointing
the twelve (6:12), he spends the night in prayer; he prays alone
to obtain Peter's confession of who he is (9:18); he becomes
transfigured during intense prayer (9:28). His example of prayer
prompts his disciples to ask him to teach them to pray (11:1-4);
at the last supper he prays that the devil will not overcome Peter
and that he will afterwards strengthen others (22:31-32); all these

prayers are effectively answered.

In the Acts of the Apostles, Jesus' successors continue the same tradition of prayer. Through Jesus' death, believers felt they had a full share in the kingdom. This meant the presence of the Spirit and the continued intercession of Jesus to the Father. Consequently, we find impressive examples of individual and community prayer in Luke's second volume. We will not include examples of the use of Jesus' name in prayer, because we have already done so.

Examples of prayer in Acts are the following: on Peter's arrest, the whole church gathered together for prayer; evidence of response came not only with Peter's miraculous escape but also with the whole house being shaken by the Spirit (4:31). Stephen's dying prayer, "Lord do not hold this sin against them," seems modeled on that of Jesus and brings about the conversion of Paul (7:57-8:3). Paul prays before his baptism and gift of the Spirit (9:11,17). An angel tells Cornelius, "Your prayers and alms have ascended as a memorial before God" (10:4). Peter is praying before being enlightened about receiving the Gentiles (10:9). In the midst of community worship and prayer, the Spirit chooses Paul for a new world apostolate (13:1-3).

Thus Luke's community could receive special encouragement and *certainty* about their own prayers, especially as they faced persecution and difficult choices. Jesus' own prayers had made it possible for others to go ahead, even in impossible circumstances. Now this same prayer, since they were together with him in his kingdom, would be their own. This made it possible to consider their own prayers those of Jesus and to look for the same certain response he received.

The Cosmic Struggle With Satan and the Christian Combat

The whole atmosphere in Luke's drama of the cross is that of a great cosmic struggle. The author mentions the darkness and eclipse of the sun to show that these are the earthshaking events before the last day of the Lord predicted by the prophet Joel (2:19-21). These seem to have a diabolical nature in view of Jesus' terrifying final triple temptation that parallels his opening temptation by the devil. Luke tells us that Satan entered Judas to set in motion the whole train of events leading to Jesus' death, and that he allied himself with the chief priests and captains (22:3-4). This is part of a whole atmosphere of intrigue in which the devil is conspiring and at work. Consequently, when Jesus is arrested by the same "chief priests and captains" (22:52) he can truly say, "This is your hour and the power of darkness" (22:53).

In this way, Luke presents his audience with a model for Christian combat so they can learn how Jesus was victorious and follow his example. This path starts with Satan's opening temptation. Luke introduces this by providing the genealogy of Jesus all the way back to Adam, who is called the "Son of God" (3:38). This hints that the struggle of Adam with the serpent in the garden of Eden is parallel to that of Jesus and can be better understood in comparison with it.

The above designation of Adam as son of God connects to Jesus' temptations in regard to "son of God" that immediately follow. The tempter twice begins by with the words, "If you are Son of God" (4:3,9). In the garden, the devil (in the NT view "the ancient serpent" [Apoc 20:2]), tempted Adam to eat a forbidden fruit just as the devil tempted Jesus to eat a bread of power that he was not to eat according to God's plans. In the garden, Satan suggests to Adam he can avoid death by following his plans and eating the forbidden fruit. In parallel, in the third temptation of Jesus, the devil tempts him to jump off the Temple pinnacle and escape death by falsely trusting God will save him.

Another parallel to Adam and the garden is the following: God gave Adam rule and authority over all the earth (1:26); the devil promises to make Jesus like Adam in having authority and power over all the earth (3:6-8). At the end, Luke notes that the devil departed from Jesus until an opportune time. This seems to be especially on the Mount of Olives where Jesus awaits Judas and the others coming to arrest him. In that story, we first of all notice that Luke's narrative begins and ends with the theme of temptation or struggle: At the beginning, Jesus says to his disciples, "Pray that you may not enter into temptation," and at the end he says, "Rise and pray that you do not enter into temptation" (22:39,46).

This opening and ending on the temptation motif provides the key to Luke's version of Jesus' prayer on the Mount of Olives. It is the resumption of Jesus' conflict with the evil one in the desert after his baptism that was broken off after Jesus' first victory (4:1-3). Luke skillfully shows this by some notable changes he makes from one of his sources, Mark 14:32-42. In Mark, Jesus was "greatly distressed and troubled;" in fact, "his soul was sorrowful even to death." In Luke's version, all these expressions of Jesus' fear and hesitation are omitted. Instead it is the disciples who are "sleeping for sorrow" (22:45). This "sorrow" has the sense of grief or despair in contrast with Jesus' confident struggle. That is why he warns them twice to pray that they may not enter into temptation, for on their own strength they could never win a struggle with what Jesus calls "the power of darkness" (22:53).

The conflict theme and parallel to the Adam–Satan encounter emerges even stronger in 22:43-44. While these verses are lacking in many Greek manuscripts, they do have prominent textual witnesses; they also fit into Luke's overall theme and thus could very well be authentic.:

> And there appeared to him an angel from heaven, strengthening him. And being in an agony, he prayed more earnestly; and his sweat became like great drops of blood falling down upon the ground.

The angel's appearance fits into the picture of a struggle with the devil, also an angelic being. The angels, according to a tradition in Apoc 12:7, fought with Satan and his cohorts, finally ejecting them from heaven. On earth, they assist human beings in a similar struggle. "Being in an agony, he prayed more earnestly" — the English word "agony" does not correspond fully with the Greek *agōnia*, which means a sharp conflict. The words "sweat" and "earth" remind us again of the garden of Eden parallels. There God told Adam:

> In the *sweat* of your face you shall eat bread till you return to the *earth*, for out of it you were taken. (Gen 3:19)

All these Adam–Jesus parallels would invite the audience to face their own temptations and struggles with new confidence since they now have a leader and model in a new Adam who can lead them to victory.

This combat theme is also found in other places in Luke, leading up to the passion narrative: Jesus sends out the twelve with "power and authority over the demons" (9:1). When seventy other apostles return, they exclaim, "Even the demons are subject to us in your name!" (10:17). Jesus replied, "I saw Satan fall like lightning from heaven" (10:17). A sign of the kingdom of heaven is that Jesus casts out devils by the finger of God (11:20). Also, Jesus cures a stooped over woman on the Sabbath and says, "Ought not this woman, a daughter of Abraham whom Satan bound for eighteen years, be loosed from this bond on the sabbath day?" (13:16)

Jesus' initial temptation and the above notices prepare the way for the final death struggle on the cross where Jesus is faced with the triple temptation to show he is Christ by coming down from the cross to save himself and others. We have noted its diabolical nature in parallel to the desert temptations. The signal of final victory is Jesus' words to the repentant criminal, "Truly I say to you, today you will be with me in Paradise" (23:43). The word Paradise, *paradeisos*, is the same word found in the Greek bible for the garden in which Adam and Eve were placed. After their fall, God drove them out and prevented their return

to Paradise by placing cherubim with a flaming sword at the entry
to the garden (Gen 3:42). In contrast, Jesus through a victorious
struggle reopens the gates of Paradise.

In the Acts of the Apostles, Luke's audience finds a continu-
ation of the same cosmic struggle. The same battle must now
be fought and won by Jesus' successors. Jesus becomes the new
Adam, source of life and victory for his followers. Peter addresses
the Temple crowds as follows,

> You denied the holy and righteous one and asked
> for a murderer to be granted to you; and killed the
> author of life whom God raised from the dead. (3:14)

The word *leader* or author of life in the Greek is *archēgon* and
brings out a contrast between Jesus, author of life, and Adam,
leader of death. The same term is used by Peter in his trial before
the council and high priest:

> The God of our fathers raised Jesus whom you killed
> by hanging him on a tree. God exalted him at his right
> hand as *Leader* and Savior to give repentance to Israel
> and forgiveness of sins. (5:30-31)

The following are some examples of the struggle against the
dark powers in the Acts of the Apostles: Peter and the apostles
cure those with "unclean spirits" who are brought to them (5:16).
Paul, in the name of Jesus, ordered a "divining spirit" to leave
a young woman who was possessed by it (16:18). The news
of the power of Christian exorcists at Ephesus brought about
many conversions due to the story of the disaster that overtook
Jewish exorcists who tried to use Jesus' name as a magic power
(19:13-20). In his final trial before King Agrippa and the Roman
governor Festus, Paul describes his mission as challenge to the
powers of darkness: "that they may turn from darkness to light
and from the power of Satan to God" (26:18).

Notes for a Modern Audience

The theme of wrestling with superhuman dark powers is a stumbling block for many modern listeners, yet it belongs to the core of the gospel. When early believers prayed, "Lead us not into temptation, but deliver us from evil," they had especially in mind the *evil one* whose power no human being could cope with. While philosophers may speculate about the personal nature of the "evil one," the reality and power of the forces of evil in this world are beyond speculation. The consistent gospel teaching is that we cannot resist temptation without a prayerful *agōnia* like that of Jesus.

4

John

The Death of Jesus and The Mystery of the Seven Signs

John employs a series of seven mysterious signs to lead his audience to a unique new appreciation of the death of Jesus. These signs are progressive and interrelated. The author starts with the changing of water to wine at Cana, which he calls the first sign: "This first of signs Jesus did at Cana in Galilee and manifested his glory" (2:11). A series of signs seems to be in mind since the raising of the dying son of the Cana official is numbered as second. John writes, "This was now the second sign that Jesus did when he came from Judea to Galilee" (4:54).

Many biblical commentaries have enumerated John's principal seven signs as follows: (1) the wedding at Cana (2:1-12); (2) the raising of the dying son of the royal official (4:46-54); (3) the Sabbath healing of the paralytic (5:1-18); (4) the multiplication of loaves (6:1-15); (5) Jesus' walking on water (6:16-22); (6) the Sabbath healing of the blind man (9:1-40); and (7) the restoration of Lazarus to life (11:1-54).

However, ancient literature did not usually use the modern logical sequences to which we are accustomed. They often made use of what is called a *chiasmus* or "ladder" to focus on the central meaning of their works. By way of illustration, let us take the series one to seven in the form of such a chiasm. This is what it would look like:

1

    2

        3

            4

        5

    6

7

In this type of arrangement (4) would be the center of meaning with all the others contributing toward it especially the beginning (1) and the end (7). One and seven would be interrelated and complete one another with (3) and (5) as well as (6) and (2) being in parallel. With this type of literary arrangement in mind, M. Girard has suggested the following structure of the seven principal signs in the gospel of John:.

(1) The wedding feast at Cana (2:1-12)
  (2) The raising of the dying son of the official (4:46-54)
    (3) The Sabbath healing at Bethesda (5:1-16)
      (4) The loaves' multiplication and the bread of life (6:1-71)
    (5) The Sabbath healing of the blind man (9:1-41)
  (6) The raising of Lazarus (11:1-41)
(7) The hour of Jesus and the issue of blood and water
(19:25-38)

In presenting this structure in contrast to the usual sequence provided in many books, M. Girard accepts R. E. Brown's definition of a sign: a prodigious deed with strong symbolic possibility that illustrates Jesus' salvific message. In view of this definition, Jesus' walking on water, often presented as a principal sign, simply does not fit. Instead, it appears to be part of the loaves' total message, perhaps emphasizing a Passover context. Second, the actual use of the word "sign" is another indication. The walking on water episode does not contain this word in contrast to all the others: 2:11; 4:54; 6:2 (referring to the previous healing at Bethesda); 9:16; 12:18 (referring to the raising up of Lazarus).

What arguments does Girard propose that the seventh sign would be the death of Jesus and the unusual flow of watery blood from his side? First of all, there is no really strong reason to conclude the signs (as in many books) with the so-called end of the book of signs in 12:37-50. The author does state, "Though he had done so many signs before them, yet they did not believe in him" (12:37). However, this statement means only that these previous signs were not enough and something more was needed. This view is strengthened by the evangelist's concluding statement after Jesus' death that "these (signs) have been written that you may believe that Jesus is the Christ, the Son of God" (20:31).

Another important indication is the special attention the gospel author gives to the accompanying issue of blood and water from Jesus' side. The disciple who saw this considered it so extraordinary that he proclaimed himself to be an eyewitness relating it so others might believe as well (19:35). Consequently, the first six signs are incomplete and point to the seventh at Jesus' "hour" when he will be lifted up and draw everyone to himself (12:32-33). In this text, Jesus refers to his death using the word *sēmainōn*, ("signing"). In addition, the author uses the word "signs" in this conclusion statement in 20:30. He could hardly be referring here only to the incomplete signs of chapters one to twelve.

I would also suggest that the passover connections are so strong in Jesus' death that the writer presumed his readers to surely know that all the passover's meaning came to a climax with the "sign of the blood" of the passover lamb: "The blood shall be a sign for you, upon the houses where you are: and when I see the blood, I will pass over you, and no plague shall fall upon you to destroy you" (Ex 12:13). Also, when the Jews ask Jesus for a sign in 2:18, he responds that it will be in destroying the Temple and raising it up, which the writer explains as referring to Jesus' body (2:21). This statement seems to hint about the seventh sign at the cross which is to come.

If we take a look back at the diagram of the suggested chiasmic structure, we immediately notice the general correspondences: (3) and (5) are both Sabbath healings; (2) and (6) contain similar death to life themes because of Jesus' word. (1) and (7) complement one another as beginning and end: Jesus' mother is found in both; the Cana wine is made possible by obedience to Jesus' word, just as Jesus obeys his Father by taking the bitter wine on the cross before dying; the Cana statement "my hour has not yet come" points to the cross for completion. The sign of the loaves appears in the central part of the ladder structure with all the other signs pointing toward it and completing its meaning, especially (1) and (7).

In addition, I would add that the most severe crisis of the gospel occurs this point: many of Jesus' disciples part from him because of his difficult saying about eating his flesh and drinking his blood (6:60-61). Jesus then points to sign seven as necessary for understanding: "What if you were to see the Son of man ascending where he was before? It is the spirit that gives life, the flesh is of no use" (6:62-63). Finally, as an added confirmation of centrality, the confession of Peter takes place at this point as an affirmation of belief in Jesus despite his difficult saying.

If the fourth sign of the loaves above is so central, it will be an important key for the implicit audience in looking for the meaning of Jesus' death. It will also help us if we understand that the writer often refers to a later event within an earlier one to illustrate its meaning. For example, the evangelist brings out that the resurrection of Lazarus is only made possible by the rising of Jesus who is the source of resurrection and life: "I am the resurrection and the life" (11:26). In another example, Jesus announces at the feast of Booths that anyone who thirsts should come to him and drink. In the next verse, the author explains that this will happen only when the Spirit comes after Jesus' glorification (7:37-38). In regard to the loaves' sign, Jesus says that his flesh and blood are real food and drink (6:55-56), but explains that this will only be understood at the lifting up of the son of Man (6:62-63).

The unique elements common to signs (1), (7) and (4) will also be important clues in our search for the special meaning of the loaves' sign as connected with Jesus' death. Only these three signs mention Jesus' mother (at Cana, 2:1-6; 6:42 in most manuscripts; at the foot of the cross, 19:25-27). Jesus' blood is mentioned only in the seventh sign as flowing from his side after his death (19:34), in the fourth sign about drinking his blood (6:52-54) and in the symbolic wine or "blood of the grape" at Cana. In all three signs there is a central theme of obedience: Jesus' taking the cup of sour wine on the cross (19:29-30), acceptance of Jesus' difficult word about eating his flesh and drinking his blood (6:51-56) and finally, obeying Jesus' words at Cana that culminate in the tasting of the new wine by the chief steward (2:10).

The evangelist's careful structure appears directed to answering important questions about the meaning of the loaves' sign, especially Jesus' most difficult saying about eating his flesh and blood, which is even repeated three times to emphasize its importance (6:52-56). Some of these questions are the following: 1) Many people misunderstood the multiplication of the loaves and thought it signified the arrival of a prophet and leader like Moses. Jesus had to flee to a mountain because he feared they would try to make him a king (6:13-14). Thus, in terms of bread, some people may have thought of Jesus as a miracle and sign-worker like Moses who gave Israel a "wonder-bread" (Exod 16:1-31). Jesus responded that Moses did not give them the true bread from heaven; only the Son of Man will provide that for them (6:27).

2) A second question flows from this: if Jesus wishes to give them a heavenly bread as Son of Man, how can this be reconciled with his obvious humanity and family ties with his mother and father (6:41-42)? In other words, how can he really have a divine

or heavenly origin if his earthly descent is so evident? Therefore, "the Jews" ask, "How does he say, 'I have come down from heaven'?" 3) The third question arises during a rather heated dispute in the audience about Jesus' words, "The bread I will give is my flesh for the life of the world" (6:51). If we follow the view that 6:51-58 refers especially to the Eucharist, the audience's reaction seems to reflect a division in the early church about the meaning of the Eucharist (Brown, 1979:74).

The expressions "eating flesh" and "drinking blood" are strong statements not only of Jesus' humanity, but also of his death. This creates such a stumbling block for his disciples that many abandon Jesus because of this difficult teaching and no longer follow him (6:60,66). Jesus has to repeat a third time that it is the bread of the Son of Man (6:27,53,62). In addition, he explains that to understand his words, they must see the Son of Man ascend to where he was before so they will know that his words are spirit and life, not flesh alone (6:62-63). Therefore, the promised bread is connected with Jesus' death and glorification together with the gift of the Spirit.

We can sum up briefly some questions raised by the fourth sign of the loaves whose answer the audience may find in the first and seventh signs: (1) Are the loaves a miraculous bread given by Jesus, a second Moses and wonderworker? (2) If the bread is a "bread from heaven" is the Jesus behind this bread also divine, and come down from heaven? (3) Can Jesus at the same time be so human and subject to death that he can give his flesh and blood?

How can all this be possible? This raises questions as to whether he really died and whether his death can be connected to the spirit and life that he promised. We will turn first to the seventh sign to see what answers it provides the audience about Jesus' sayings on the loaves, especially the most difficult statement about eating his flesh and drinking his blood.

The Seventh Sign (19:25-37), the Water and Blood from Jesus' Side: "The sign shall be the blood" (Exod 12:13)

> But standing by the cross of Jesus were his mother, and his mother's sister, Mary the wife of Clopas, and Mary Magdalene. When Jesus saw his mother, and the disciple whom he loved standing near, he said to his mother, "Woman, behold, your son!" Then he said to the disciple, "Behold, your mother!" And from that hour the disciple took her to his own home. (19:25-27)

First of all, why should the seventh sign start with the above verses? The author starts with 19:25 because he must first introduce key witnesses to the coming essential saving event. These witnesses are especially the mother of Jesus and the beloved disciple. Both of them will actually see Jesus die, and also witness the extraordinary flow of blood and water from Jesus' side. The evangelist considers this so important that he states that he is a chosen witness who knows what he says is true and that he relates it so that others may believe also (19:35). The pericope comes to a natural end with the scripture quotations that follow his witness in 19:36-37. The final quote has, "They shall look on him whom they have pierced," which is a fitting conclusion to the "looking on" of the chosen witnesses above.

The question of the historicity of the presence of Mary and the Beloved Disciple need not detain us, even though neither is present in the synoptic gospels' accounts. The evangelist uses the words "see" and "know" in deeper senses. Even the blind can "see" if they really hear Jesus' words (9:39). By the time the gospel is written, Jesus' mother has been certainly dead for many years, yet the author writes as if the events are of present significance to his audience in his witness (19:35). The evangelist regards the events at the cross not as past history but as part of a timeless drama. For example, Jesus always bears the marks of the cross on his hands, and the wound in his side (20:20,25).

This view is also found elsewhere in the NT. For example, Paul states that he presented the Galatians with a crucified Christ, although years after the events (3:1). However in this study, we are not concerned with synoptic comparisons or recovering original historical situations. We are taking the gospel of John as a literary whole that made sense to the writer (and his audience) in the form that he left it to them.

In presenting Jesus' mother and the beloved disciple as witnesses, the author is trying to trace a direct link to Jesus. This is to establish his credibility for his audience and community in regard to the teachings he is presenting. The words of Jesus to his mother "Woman, behold your son," and to the beloved disciple, "Behold your mother," (19:27) can bear a wide range of meaning, especially in regard to symbolism. However, M. DeGoedt has suggested that the words, "Behold your mother" are a revelatory formula introducing a special new role as a mother that Mary will exercise in regard to the beloved disciple and his community. The words cannot be limited to simply a last command on Jesus' part that a favorite disciple continue the care of his mother; any interpretation must also keep in mind the role that "the disciple whom Jesus loved" has for the audience of the gospel.

The exact identification of this beloved disciple may forever elude the scriptural scholar; however, we can readily understand that it would be very important for the author of the fourth gospel or the source behind it to establish a direct link with Jesus for the benefit of his audience or community. A line of succession in authentic teaching could be established only by making as close a connection as possible to Jesus. Consequently, a last word of Jesus affirming a relationship between his mother and the beloved disciple would be extremely important. It would establish him as a "brother of the Lord" with authority like that of James, Jesus' blood relative, and other disciples of Jesus, even Peter. R. E. Brown writes, "By stressing not only that his mother has become the mother of the beloved disciple, but also that the disciple has become her son, the Johannine Jesus is logically claiming the disciple as his true brother" (1979:74).

However, P. Minear has brought out the important scriptural parallel of Benjamin as the beloved son of Jacob. This invites us to consider the beloved disciple as a favorite son or protege of Jesus, who then continues on as "adopted" by Mary. This picture of favorite son is confirmed by the parallel between Jesus in the Father's bosom (1:18) and the beloved disciple reclining on Jesus' bosom (13:23). Yet whether we take the brother or favorite son image, the succession motif implied would be very important for the writer in view of his witness and explanation of these singular events.

Returning to the questions about the loaves in sign (4), we can now study how they are answered in sign (7) as witnessed by Mary and the beloved disciple. One question concerned the origin of the bread (and Jesus) from heaven: "The Jews then murmured at him, because he said, 'I am the bread which has come down from heaven' " (6:42). To answer this, the witnesses at the cross pay special attention to the manner in which Jesus died: he seemed to know exactly when he was going to die: when he took the sour wine, he bowed his head and said, "It is finished" (19:30). Finally, he appeared deliberately to bow his head and expire (19:30).

This manner of death was anticipated in 10:18 where Jesus stated that no one would take his life away from him; he would die by choice with the power to give (lay down) his life and take it up again in view of the command of his Father. All this points to something above-human in Jesus' death. It is surely real, but no human being has the power to determine when life will come and when it will go. The gospel's prologue indicated that the Word came into the world at his own choice, and now he dies in the same manner. Thus there is a divine element in Jesus which confirms that the bread that he gives comes down, like himself, from heaven. Therefore, the chosen witnesses can affirm that his manner of death has answered the question about the loaves in sign (4): "How does he now say I have come down from heaven?"

(6:42).

The hardest question of all concerns Jesus' difficult statement about the necessity of eating his flesh and drinking his blood (John 6:52-56). This question produced a dramatic crisis in discipleship. To answer this, the chosen witnesses, especially Jesus' mother and the beloved disciple, affirm the reality of Jesus' humanity and death. They saw that the soldiers found him dead and did not consider it necessary to break his bones as they did with the others to hasten their death. In addition, the lethal spear thrust followed by an issue of blood and water was an added guarantee of death.

However, this means only that he surely died. It is not enough to show how his death could have made it possible for believers to eat his flesh and drink his blood. Yet there is a hint of special meaning in the words, "He bowed his head and gave up the spirit" (19:30). These words of themselves mean nothing more than that he expired or died. However, in view of the next incident, and of the whole gospel, the phrase may symbolize that Jesus "gave up the spirit" for others to others. For added indications, we must study carefully the following unusual incident since those words alone are not enough.

> But when they came to Jesus and saw that he was already dead, they did not break his legs. But one of the soldiers pierced his side with a spear, and at once there came out blood and water. He who saw it has borne witness — his witness is true, and he knows that he tells the truth — that you also may believe. (19:32-35)

The supreme moment of the seventh sign is the piercing of Jesus' side, and (what the author considers) a most unusual resulting flow of blood and water. The evangelist places so much significance on this that he cites the words of the eyewitness who relates the incident, emphasizes its truth, and tells it that others may also believe as he did (19:35). What does the writer see in this event? He does not immediately tell us, but we will see that he connects it with an important promise of Jesus and with God's plan in the scriptures.

In regard to the first way, Jesus' word or prediction, he had promised on the last day of the feast of Booths, "If anyone thirst, let him come [to me (in most texts)] and let him drink who believes in me. As the Scripture says, 'From within him shall flow rivers of living water' " (7:37-38). This is the translation of R. E. Brown in his commentary on John (1966:320-322). There he details his reasons for understanding the second half ("from within him," etc.) as referring to Jesus rather than to the believer. However, regardless of which translation, the evangelist in the next verse does note that Jesus was speaking of the spirit that those who believed in him were to receive, and that this spirit would only come at Jesus' glorification.

The customs of the feast of Booths add special significance to Jesus' words: Every day for seven days there was special procession of water to the temple where the priest poured a bowl of water and a bowl of wine on the altar. On the seventh day the priests went around the altar seven times before doing so. These actions aroused messianic hopes for the future since the prophet Zechariah had announced that all the nations would one day come up to Jerusalem to worship on that feast (14:16). The combination of water and wine on this occasion may also have been in the evangelist's mind as important parallels to Cana and the cross.

Consequently, the surprising flow of bloody water from Jesus' side could be understood as confirming Jesus' words that his glorification on the cross would bring the gift of the spirit/water as a result of his bloody sacrifice. This would also fulfill Jesus' words during the fourth sign of the loaves that they would understand his difficult words about flesh and blood in terms of spirit and life once they *see* the son of Man ascending into heaven (6:62,63). The witnessing disciple seems to be connecting with this statement when he emphasizes that he *saw* the water, symbolizing spirit, coming from Jesus side, which was a sign that he had ascended into heaven.

We have thus pointed out that the extraordinary flow of water and blood from Jesus' side fulfills his promise about being the source of the Spirit, and that his words about flesh and blood were to be understood in terms of the spirit and life. However, this does not explain how *eating* his flesh and drinking his blood should be connected to his death. This explanation will take place through the author's presentation of Jesus' death as a paschal lamb sacrifice. A key to this are the central moments in the passover ritual celebration in Exodus 12. These are *eating* of the paschal lamb and taking upon themselves the "sign of the blood" which God would *see* sprinkled on their houses and thus save them from death.

In what follows, we will present indications that the writer was presenting his audience an image of Jesus as the new paschal lamb sacrifice whose flesh is to be eaten by believers, and whose blood is to be the source of their life.

First of all, the author carefully describes Jesus' passion and death in a passover setting, especially in regard to eating the passover lamb. This eating is central to the passover ritual in Exodus 12 where it is mentioned six times. Accordingly, John notes that the Jews could not enter Pilate's pretorium, "so they might not be defiled, but might *eat* the passover" (18:28). Also, he mentions that Jesus was condemned and led away on "the day of Preparation of the Passover; it was about the sixth hour" (19:14); this would be the time when the passover lambs were to led away to slaughter, since they all had to be sacrificed before the evening (Exod 12:22).

In addition, the evangelist's mention of the hyssop and the basin at the foot of the cross (19:29; Exod 12:22) are passover features, for the "sign of the blood" was sprinkled on the houses by a hyssop dipped in a basin. Finally, the author notes twice that it was the preparation day for the passover in regard to Jesus' body remaining on the cross and being buried (19:31,42). From a literary standpoint, the description of the end of Jesus' life links with the beginnings of his ministry where John the Baptist had first introduced Jesus with the words, "Behold the Lamb of God who takes away the sin of the world" (1:29) and "Behold the Lamb of God" (1:35). In both circumstances, John the Baptist *saw* Jesus or looked at him when he said these words, just as the disciple *saw* the bloody flow from Jesus' side that showed he was the paschal lamb of God (19:35). Thus the links between beginning and end of the gospel would be important audience cues.

Within this passover setting, most striking is the description of Jesus' death in terms of a passover lamb sacrifice whose flesh is to be eaten and whose blood will bring life. The first element in any sacrifice, especially that of the passover lamb, was that all should be done in obedience to God. The passover ritual is prescribed in detail by God's own words (Ex 12:1), and it is noted that the people did exactly as he said: "Then the people of Israel went and did so; as the Lord had commanded Moses and Aaron, so they did" (12:28). Consequently, the author stresses Jesus' obedience to the Father right until his last breath. The way was already prepared for this when Jesus stated at his arrest, "Shall I not drink the cup which the Father has given me?" (18:11).

To apply the above words literally, the author writes, "After this, Jesus, knowing that all was now finished, said (to fulfill the scripture), 'I thirst' " (19:28). The author describes Jesus as consciously saying these words in view of the scriptural plan of Ps 69:21, "In my thirst they gave me bitter wine to drink." There seems to be a special emphasis on this *oxos*, or bitter wine of Ps 69:21, which is here repeated three times (19:28-30). Jesus seems to be taking this as a final act of obedience, for the writer notes that after Jesus had taken the bitter wine, he said, "It is finished" and then bowed his head and expired (19:30). It is possible that this bowing of his head is also a gesture of obedience like that of the Israelites who bowed their heads after hearing all of God's words about the saving passover ritual (12:27). Later we will see in the first sign that Jesus' mother will direct the waiters to do everything that Jesus says (2:5). The "good wine" will be made possible through obedience to Jesus' word, just as he has obeyed his Father right to the end by accepting the "bitter wine."

The second element in portraying Jesus' death as a passover sacrifice to be consumed is found in the events that took place on the cross which the writer understands as fulfilling God's plan in the scriptures. First of all, he notes that, strangely enough, the soldiers did not break Jesus' legs as they did with the other two crucified. He sees this as accomplishing the Scriptural prescriptions for the *eating* of the paschal lamb: "In one house shall it be eaten; you shall not carry any of the flesh outside the house; and you shall not break a bone" (Exod 12:46). It should be noted that the flesh of the lamb is mentioned in Exod 12:8 with the words, "You shall eat the flesh that night." This would correspond to Jesus' words in the loaves sign, 6:51, where he speaks of eating his flesh. The Greek of Exod 12:8 uses *ta krea* for the flesh, and also in 12:46, but the *sarx* root used by Jesus in 6:51-56 is also used of the flesh of sacrifice in Lev 4:11 and in 17:11 where it is written that the "life of the flesh is in the blood."

The final part of the passover nature of Jesus' death concerns the passover blood which is the essential element: "The blood shall be a sign for you, upon the houses where you are; and when I *see* the blood, I will pass over you. . ."(Exod 12:13). The writer emphasizes that he has *seen* this blood flow from the side of Christ: "And at once there came out blood and water. He who saw it has borne witness — his testimony is true, and he knows that he tells the truth — that you also may believe" (19:35). This flow of blood is extremely important for him because the actual *flow* of blood was required in Jewish law for a valid sacrifice.

The author recognizes all this as a fulfillment of God's plan found in the Scriptures, for he notes, "And again another scripture says, 'They shall look on him whom they have pierced'" (19:37; Zech 12:1 according to some Hebrew mss). Immediately preceding this in Zechariah we find, "I will pour out on the house of David and on the inhabitants of Jerusalem a spirit of grace and petition." Several verses later we have, "On that day there shall be open to the house of David and the inhabitants of Jerusalem a fountain to purify from sin and uncleanness" (MT Zech 13:1).

Blood of course was necessary for any purification from sin, of which the text speaks. The fact that the word "fountain" is used in the texts is significant since this is the common word for a drinking source, which would correspond to Jesus' words about drinking his blood (6:51-56). The Hebrew root behind "pierce" is *dakar*, or "thrust through" which is usually a mortal wound. Putting all together, the writer finds a perfect parallel of Jesus to the passover lamb sacrifice. In obedience to the Father, Jesus drank the bitter wine, "blood of the grape". Therefore, his life/blood became a sacrifice, a prayer-offering to God for forgiveness and life, just as the blood of the Passover lambs sprinkled on Jewish homes saved the people from destruction by the Egyptians at the time of the Exodus (12:23) and brought them life.

To sum up: We have seen that the seventh sign presents the extraordinary flow of water and blood from Jesus' side as a sure indication to the audience that Jesus is indeed the new passover. Central to the passover was the eating of the lamb and the "sign of the blood." By the passover atmosphere, and the descriptions of Jesus' death in terms of passover eating regulations, the writer explains the meaning of Jesus' words in the loaves sign that his flesh is to be eaten. The flow of water and blood fulfill Jesus' predictions as well as a scriptural plan that he will be the source of the spirit after his death. Thus he also fulfills the prediction in 6:62-63 that his glorification will show his words about his flesh and blood must be understood in terms of spirit and life. The flow of Jesus' blood corresponds to the sacrificial flow of the passover lamb's blood which brought life to the Israelites. It is thus a source of life for the audience of believers, and confirms Jesus' words in the loaves sign about the necessity of his blood as well as his flesh.

However, the gospel audience must learn how they can actually be united to Jesus by taking the flesh and blood of the new paschal lamb. Our next step will be to examine sign one, to see if it gives us any direction in this important final step. Since the original gospel audience was accustomed to chiastic arrangements, they would indeed be looking for such correspondences, especially as they listened to the gospel again and again.

The First Sign, Cana of Galilee and its Interconnected Meaning with the Fourth and Seventh Signs

> On the third day there was a marriage at Cana in Galilee, and the mother of Jesus was there; Jesus also was invited to the marriage, with his disciples. When the wine gave out, the mother of Jesus said to him, "They have no wine." And Jesus said to her, "O woman, what have you to do with me. My hour has not yet come."

We would expect a close relationship between the first and seventh signs: the last is hidden in the first and the first completes the last so that both together bring out the full meaning of the fourth sign of the loaves, especially Jesus' saying about eating his flesh and drinking his blood. On the surface, there are common elements in both first and seventh sign: Jesus' mother, the "hour" of Jesus, the thirst or lack of wine, the obedience motif, the wine/blood/water.

The Cana story begins with Jesus' mother present at a wedding, and with Jesus and his disciples also invited. In the corresponding seventh sign, the presence of Jesus' mother was important as a witness of succession and tradition along with the beloved disciple. Of course, a wedding is a well-known symbol of the messianic days (Is 54:4-8; 66:4-5). The wedding and the banquet are symbols used elsewhere by Jesus (Matt 8:11; 9:15; 22:1-14). Abundant wine was the essential ingredient of such celebrations, and to run short on such an occasion would be a long-remembered embarrassment for a married couple. But we shall note that the meaning of the story goes far beyond any original setting and contains directions to show how the believer /audience can celebrate the messianic banquet.

The embarrassing shortage of wine prompts Mary to bring up the matter privately to Jesus, saying, "They have no wine." Jesus responds (literally), "What is it to me and to you, woman? My hour has not yet come" (2:4). The expression, "What is it to me and to you" has a negative nuance. However, C. H. Giblin has demonstrated through analysis of Johannine parallels that the words do not necessarily mean a refusal to act. They imply, however, that if Jesus acts, it will be according to *his own* conscious purpose, not according to that of others. Consequently, at Cana, he will not act according to Mary's expectations or that of others, but in accord with his *hour* which will make known his true relationship with the Father and with his people.

As a result, what Jesus really wants to accomplish at Cana will be understood only through the seventh and last sign at the cross. This will also provide an answer to another question proposed at the fourth sign of the loaves. There we noted that the people misinterpreted Jesus' sign and understood him as another wonder-worker like Moses bringing miraculous bread in the desert. Jesus refused to accept this role for himself and the bread he offered. So he withdrew from the crowd, fearing they would try to make him a king (6:14). At Cana, likewise, Jesus refuses to act out of this motive, but only in view of the approaching hour on the cross and the meaning of the seventh sign.

> His mother said to the servants, "Do whatever he tells you." Now six stone jars were standing there, for the Jewish rites of purification, each holding twenty or thirty gallons. Jesus said to them, "Fill the jars with water." And they filled them to the brim. He said to them, "Now draw some out, and take it to the steward of the feast." So they took it. When the steward of the feast tasted the water now become wine, and did not

> know where it came from (though the servants who had
> drawn the water knew), the steward of the feast called
> the bridegroom and said to him, "Everyone serves the
> good wine first and when people have drunk freely,
> then the poor wine; but you have kept the good wine
> until now." (2:1-10)

After the statement about Jesus' hour, his mother tells the waiters (and the gospel audience), "Do whatever he tells you" (2:5). This appears to be an authoritative voice, in view of her special role in tradition and succession that we have seen in the seventh sign. The emphasis is on perfect obedience to Jesus' word. This is noted three times: by Mary's word, by the waiters filling the jars as Jesus directed, and by their obedience to his command to carry the jars to the chief steward. The culminating action is the chief steward's tasting of the "good wine" at the end of a chain of obedience to Jesus' commands. We note immediately the striking and intended parallel to Jesus on the cross who obeys God's plan by taking the poorer, bitter wine as the cup of suffering prepared by his Father (19:28-30; 18:11). Mary then is directing the community to obey Jesus' words, just as he has obeyed the Father's.

The wedding at Cana informs the gospel audience that the choice wine of the new age ("you have kept the good wine until now") in 2:10 can only be obtained in obedience to Jesus' words, just as the parallel blood/water/spirit from Jesus' side was only made possible by his acceptance of the imperfect, bitter "blood of the grape" on the cross in obedience to the Father. The community must participate in Jesus' hour and its meaning if they wish to receive the choice wine and Spirit made available by his death. There may also be an intended parallel to Jesus who accepts "the poor wine" of the old age on the cross so that the "good wine" may be kept for the new age.

The story also hints at the ritual way this is to be done. Mary tells the waiters (and the gospel audience), "Do whatever he tells you." This whole process of obedience to Jesus culminates with the chief steward taking the cup of new wine, just as Jesus took the bitter wine on the cross in obedience to his father. We have noted that this was linked with the cup statement of 18:11, "Shall I not drink the cup which the Father has given me?" This would point to the importance of taking the cup/wine in obedience to Jesus' words. It would also be in obedience to his words in the fourth sign that it was necessary to drink his blood in order to have everlasting life (6:53-55). While there is no mention of eating Jesus' flesh or bread at Cana, it is quite possible that the author understood that the taking of the cup was primary, or that it included both. It could include both in view of the scriptural statement, "The life of the flesh is in the blood" (Lev 17:11). If this is so, we can suggest that the taking of the cup, in imitation of Jesus, was primary for John and his audience.

In sum, the first sign completes the fourth and seventh by providing a ritual means for the community/audience to be united to Jesus, the new sacrificial paschal lamb. The authority of Jesus' mother directs them to obey Jesus' words. This finally leads to taking of the cup of "good wine" by the chief steward. It also directs them to obey Jesus' words in the fourth sign about drinking his blood. The taking of the cup at Jesus' command seems primary for John's audience as the way of joining themselves to Jesus as paschal sacrifice.

Final Conclusion

John's drama of Jesus' death centers the audience's attention on Jesus as the new Passover, especially in regard to the passover meal. In this meal, the meaning of Jesus' statement about consuming his flesh and blood can be understood. The author brings this out through a literary interconnection between the central sign of the loaves (6:1-71), the first sign of Cana (2:1-12) and a final sign on the cross culminating with the extraordinary flow of blood and water from Jesus' side. Thus, questions raised about Jesus' bread in the sign of the loaves, especially the difficult statement of eating his flesh and drinking his blood, can be answered through the first and last signs. The seventh or last sign affirms Jesus' divinity, his humanity and his sacrificial death as the new passover lamb. The scriptural allusions and setting, especially the unusual flow of water and blood from Jesus' side, affirm that he is indeed the Passover lamb that takes away the sins of the world, and that he must be "eaten" by the believer/audience.

The author draws special attention to the Passover "sign of the blood" and Jesus' obedience to his Father on the cross in his acceptance of the bitter wine to fulfill the Scriptures. Consequently, Jesus' words about eating his flesh and drinking his blood find their meaning in the passover setting of the last "sign" in 19:25-37. The first sign at Cana completes the picture by providing a way for the community to participate through a ritual action. Jesus' mother directs them to obey Jesus' words just as he has obeyed those of his Father. Just as Jesus took the bitter cup of wine as a final act of obedience to the father, they must obey his words about "drinking his blood" and take the cup of "good wine" as a final mark of obedience just as the chief steward did.

Notes for a modern audience

For John's gospel, the modern audience needs to make few adaptations in listening to the drama of Jesus' death. The inner key is still the same: faith and obedience to Jesus' word, to initiate the sign or sacrament value of taking the ritual cup in celebration of the Lord's supper as a new Passover. Jesus' obedience to the Father gave infinite value to his actions on the cross and made it into a new Passover sacrifice. Likewise the audience or believers, obeying Jesus in taking the cup, can make their participation in the new Passover a most fruitful action for themselves and for the world.

Bibliography of Special Sources and Works Consulted

G. Bilezekian, *The Liberated Gospel: A Comparison of the Gospel of Mark and Greek Tragedy* (Grand Rapids: Baker, 1977)

S. G. F. Brandon, "The Date of the Markan Gospel," *NTS* 7(1961) 126-141

R. E. Brown, *The Gospel According to John* (Garden City: Doubleday, 1966)

_____. *The Community of the Beloved Disciple* (N. Y.: Doubleday, 1979)

H. L. Chronis, "The Torn Veil: Cultus and Christology in Mark 15:37-39," *JBL* 101(1982) 97-114

W. D. Davies, *The Setting of the Sermon on the Mount* (Cambridge: Cambridge Univ. Press, 1964)

T. L. Donaldson, *Jesus on the Mountain: A Study in Matthean Theology*, (JSNTSup8; Sheffield: *JSOT*, 1985)

M. DeGoedt, "Un schème de révélation dans le quatrième évangile," *Novum Testamentum* 8(1962)142-50

J. Dupont, *Les trois apocalypses synoptiques, Marc 13; Matthieu 24-25; Luc 21* (LL 121; Paris: Cerf, 1985)

P. Ellis, *The Genius of John* (Collegeville: Liturgical Press, 1984)

A. Feuillet, "Le logion sur la rançon," *RevSciPhilTheol* 51(1967) 365-402

J. Fitzmyer, *The Gospel According to Luke* (Garden City: Doubleday, 1981)

J. M. Ford, "Reconciliation and Forgiveness in Luke's Gospel," in R. J. Cassidy & P. J. Scharper, eds, *Political Issues in Luke-*

Acts (Maryknoll: Orbis, 1983)

J. M. Ford, *My Enemy Is My Guest: Jesus and Violence in Luke* (Maryknoll: Orbis, 1984)

J. Gerard, The first draft of a doctoral dissertation entitled, *The Literary Unity and the Compositional Methods of the Gospel of John* (m.d.) as used and quoted by P. Ellis.

C. Giblin, "Suggestion, Negative Response, and Positive Action in St. John's Portrayal of Jesus," *NTS* 26(1980) 197-211

M. Girard, "La composition structurelle des sept signes dans le quatrième évangile," *Sciences Religieuses* 9(1980) 315-24

J. Grassi, "Eating Jesus' Flesh and Drinking His Blood: The Centrality and Meaning of John 6:51-58," *BTB* 17(1987)24-30.

J. Grassi, *God Makes Me Laugh: A New Approach to Luke* (Wilmington: M. Glazier, 1986)

J. Grassi, *Broken Bread and Broken Bodies: The Lord's Supper and World Hunger* (Maryknoll: Orbis, 1985)

R. H. Gundry, *Matthew: A Commentary on his Literary and Theological Art* (Grand Rapids: Eerdmans, 1982). References to the Jesus-Moses theme are found in the topical index.

D. H. Hare, *The Theme of Jewish Persecution of Christians in the Gospel According to St. Matthew* (Cambridge: Cambridge Univ. Press, 1967)

M. Hengel, *The Atonement: The Origins of the Doctrine in the New Testament* (Philadelphia: Fortress, 1981)

W. Horbury, and B. McNeil, eds, *Suffering and Martyrdom in the New Testament: Studies Presented to G.M. Slyter by the Cambridge New Testament Seminar* (Cambridge: Cambridge University, 1981)

T. Howath, *The Sacrificial Interpretation of Jesus' Achievement in the New Testament* (N.Y.: Philosophical Library, 1979)

S. Johnson, *The Gospel According to St. Mark* (N.Y.: Harper & Bros., 1960)

S. Johnson, "Greek and Jewish Heroes: Fourth Maccabees and the Gospel of Mark," in *Early Christian Literature and the Classical Intellectual Tradition In Honorem Robert M. Grant*, W. Schoedel and R. Wilken, ed. (Paris: Editions Beauchesne, 1979) 155-176

D. Juel, *Messiah and Temple: The Trial of Jesus in the Gospel of Mark*, SBLDS 31 (Missoula: Scholars Press, 1977)

W. Kelber, *Mark's Story of Jesus* (Philadelphia: Fortress, 1979)

J. D. Kingsbury, *Matthew as Story* (Phila.: Fortress, 1986)

F. Matera, "The Death of Jesus according to Luke: A Question of Sources," *CBQ* 47(1985) 473-474

J. P. Meier, "Nations, or Gentiles in Matthew 28:19," *CBQ* 39(1977) 94-102. Meier supports the view that both Gentile and Jewish Christians together are invisioned by Matthew as the goal of his church.

J. P. Meier, *Matthew* (Wilmington: M. Glazier, 1981)

P. Minear, "The Beloved Disciple in the Gospel of John. Some Clues and Conjectures," *NTS* 19(1977) 105-23

J. Neyrey, *The Passion According to Luke* (N.Y.: Paulist, 1985)

J. Nolland, "Grace as Power," *NT* 28(1986) 26-31

R. F. O' Toole, *The Unity of Luke's Theology* (Wilmington: M. Glazier, 1984)

D. Rhoads, "Narrative Criticism and the Gospel of Mark," *JAAR* 50(1982) 422

D. Rhoads & D. Michie, *Mark as Story: An Introduction to the Narrative of a Gospel* (Philadelphia: Fortress, 1982)

H. Riesenfeld, *The Resurrection in Ezechiel 37 and in the Dura-Europos Paintings*, (Uppsala: Lundequistska bokhandeln, 1948)

V. Robbins, *Jesus the Teacher, A Socio-Rhetorical Intrepretation of Mark* (Philadelphia, Fortress, 1984)

H. J. Scheops, trans, D. R. A. Hare, *Jewish Christianity: Factional Disputes in the Early Church*, (Phila: Fortress, 1969)

D. Senior, " 'With Swords and Clubs' — The Setting of Mark's Community and His Critique of Abusive Power,"*BTB* 17(1987)10-20

D. Senior, "The Struggle to be Universal: Mission as a Vantage Point for New Testament Investigation" *CBQ* 46(1984) 63-81. Senior has a bibliographical discussion of other authors who have also presented this viewpoint especially in regard to Mark.

D. Senior, "The Death of Jesus and the Resurrection of the Holy Ones" (Mt 27:51-53), *CBQ* 38(1976) 312-329

D. Schmidt, "Luke's 'Innocent Jesus': A Scriptural Apologetic," in R. J. Cassidy & P. J. Scharper, eds, *Political Issues in Luke-Acts* (Maryknoll: Orbis, 1983)

R. H. Smith, "Darkness at Noon: Mark's Passion Narrative," *CTM* 44(1973) 325-338

J. Staley, "The Structure of John's Prologue: Its Implications for the Gospel's Narrative Structure," *CBQ* 48(1986) 241-264

C. H. Talbert, "Martyrdom in Luke-Acts and the Lukan Social Ethic," in R. J. Cassidy & P.J. Scharper, eds, *Political Issues in Luke-Acts* (Maryknoll: Orbis, 1983)

R. Tannehill, "The Disciples in Mark: The Function of a Narrative Role," *JR* 57(1977) 386-405

Home delivery
from
Sheed & Ward

Here's your opportunity to have bestsellers delivered right to you. Our free catalog is filled with the newest titles on spirituality, church in the modern world, women in religion, ministry, small group resources, adult education/scripture, medical ethics videos and Sheed & Ward classics.

Please send me a free Sheed & Ward catalog for home delivery.

NAME _____

ADDRESS _____

CITY _____ STATE/ZIP _____

If you have friends who would like to order books at home, we'll send them a catalog to —

NAME _____

ADDRESS _____

CITY _____ STATE/ZIP _____

NAME _____

ADDRESS _____

CITY _____ STATE/ZIP _____